GREAT
BUILDING
FEATS

THE COLOSSEUM

LESLEY A. DuTEMPLE

Lerner Publications Company
Minneapolis

The publisher gratefully acknowledges the generous assistance of Dr. Rabun M. Taylor, Assistant Professor of History of Art and Architecture, Harvard University.

Lerner Publications Company
A division of Lerner Publishing Group
241 First Avenue North
Minneapolis, MN 55401 U.S.A.

Website address: www.lernerbook.com

Library of Congress Cataloging-in-Publication Data

DuTemple, Lesley A.
    The colosseum / by Lesley A. DuTemple.
        p.   cm. — (Great building feats)
    Includes bibliographical references and index.
    ISBN: 0–8225–4693–0 (lib. bdg. : alk. paper)
    1. Colosseum (Rome, Italy)—Juvenile literature. 2. Amphitheaters—Rome—Juvenile literature. 3. Rome (Italy)—Buildings, structures, etc.—Juvenile literature. 4. Architecture, Roman—Italy—Rome—Juvenile literature. I. Title. II. Series.
    DG68.1 .D88 2003
    937'.6—dc21   2002008108

Manufactured in the United States of America
1 2 3 4 5 6 – DP – 08 07 06 05 04 03

CONTENTS

ABOUT GREAT BUILDING FEATS

HUMANS HAVE LONG SOUGHT to make their mark on the world. From the ancient Great Wall of China to the ultramodern Channel Tunnel linking Great Britain and France, grand structures reveal how people have tried to express themselves and better their lives.

Great structures have served a number of purposes. Sometimes they met a practical need. For example, the New York subway system makes getting around a huge city easier. Other structures reflected spiritual beliefs. The Pantheon in Rome, Italy, was created as a temple to Roman gods and later became a Catholic church. Sometimes we can only guess at the story behind a structure. The purpose of Stonehenge in England eludes us, and perhaps it always will.

This book is one in a series of books called Great Building Feats. Each book in the series takes a close look at one of the most amazing building feats around the world. Each of them posed a unique set of engineering and geographical problems. In many cases, these problems seemed nearly insurmountable when construction began.

The Colosseum has been a popular subject for artists for hundreds of years. The Dutch artist Gaspar van Wittel painted this view of the Colosseum in the early eighteenth century.

More than a compilation of facts, the Great Building Feats series not only describes how each structure was built but also why. Each project called forth the best minds of its time. Many people invested their all in the outcome. Their lives are as much a part of the structure as the earth and stone used in its construction. Finally, each structure in the Great Building Feats series remains a dynamic feature of the modern world, still amazing users and viewers as well as historians.

AMPHITHEATER OF DEATH

The Colosseum in Rome, Italy, is considered by many to be the most famous building in the world. It was built nearly two thousand years ago for the purpose of hosting violent gladiator games. Thousands of men, women, and animals fought for their lives on the Colosseum's sandy arena floor. A few gladiators, or warriors, found glory there. Some even found

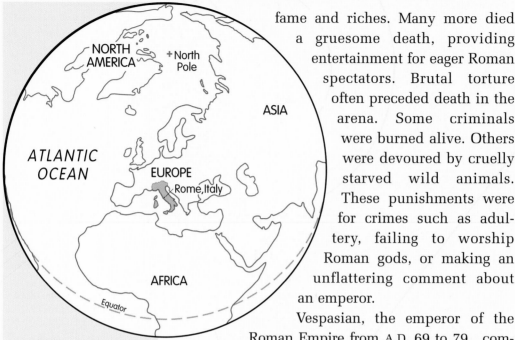

The Colosseum is in Rome, Italy. It is one of the most visited sights in the country.

fame and riches. Many more died a gruesome death, providing entertainment for eager Roman spectators. Brutal torture often preceded death in the arena. Some criminals were burned alive. Others were devoured by cruelly starved wild animals. These punishments were for crimes such as adultery, failing to worship Roman gods, or making an unflattering comment about an emperor.

Vespasian, the emperor of the Roman Empire from A.D. 69 to 79, commissioned (ordered the building of) the Colosseum. The year before he became emperor, four consecutive emperors had been murdered (or intimidated into committing suicide) for being cruel and selfish rulers. But Vespasian was a survivor. He was a leader of action and strong conscience. He also was not naive. He knew that he would have to work hard to win the favor of the Roman people, who were exhausted from the anger, poverty, and violence caused by his predecessors.

One way to gain favor was to provide the people with entertainment. Gladiator games were wildly popular among Romans, even though the city of Rome had no suitable place for holding them. The city needed an amphitheater, or arena. Vespasian decided that he would provide one as a gift to the people. He started construction on the enormous, complex Flavian Amphitheater—which later would be called the Colosseum—in about A.D. 75.

Vespasian did not live to see his amphitheater completed. After he died in 79, his oldest son, Titus, continued construction on the amphitheater. Titus opened it to the public in 80. After Titus's untimely death the following year, Domitian—Vespasian's youngest son and Titus's younger brother—built the underground caverns and finished the decorative work.

The finished building, with its soaring façade, grand arches, and tens of thousands of seats, was imposing and magnificent. Its image was stamped on coins. It was a tribute to the power and grandeur of the Roman Empire and a stunning symbol of a family's generosity. Although some parts of the building have crumbled and others have been torn down, time has not dimmed its greatness. People have studied and painted and sketched it for hundreds of years. It has survived earthquakes, devastating fires, countless wars, and more than one thousand years of neglect. Yet the Colosseum remains a magnificent structure.

It also provides a profound example of the architectural, engineering, and inventive talents of the ancient Romans. Its construction posed two serious problems—how to hold up such an enormous weight and how to allow fifty thousand people to comfortably move in, out, and around the structure. Through the use of concrete (which the Romans invented), architectural elements such as barrel vaults (which the Romans developed and refined), and a dizzying system of walkways and stairways, the architects of the Colosseum solved these problems on a grand scale. And most of the building went up in about five years, an impressive speed in any era. Thousands of workers, many of them slaves, worked on the project. It was the largest amphitheater in the world and the biggest public building project Rome had ever seen.

However beautiful and impressive, the Colosseum stands primarily as a reminder of the ancient Romans' disturbing appetite for bloodletting as entertainment. For more than four hundred years, the Colosseum was an amphitheater of death. In the centuries that have passed since then, it has gone through several transitions. It has been a church, a fortress, a quarry, a shrine, and one of the most visited tourist sights in Italy. Through all of this, however, the Colosseum has remained, more than anything else, a mute testimony to the gruesome gladiator games it once held.

IMPERIAL ARCHITECTS

Most structures that were commissioned by emperors were credited to the emperor who commissioned them, even though emperors themselves were almost never the architect. No matter how brilliant the design or how well the engineering problems were solved, it was the emperor's name that was attached to the building. The architects of the Colosseum, for example, have been forgotten.

Chapter One
THE GLADIATOR GAMES

(264 B.C.–A.D. 68)

IT WAS SUMMER, AND THE CITY of Rome was seething with excitement. The world's largest amphitheater was about to open to the public for the first time. People were thrilled by what they expected to see inside: bloody gladiator games. By order of Titus, the emperor of the Roman Empire, the opening day had been declared a public holiday that would begin with a grand procession, or parade, through the streets of Rome. Posters announcing the

Lictors (government officials) parade through the streets of Rome.

inaugural festivities had been plastered all over the city. Titus had invited people from all reaches of the empire to join in the celebration, and Rome was filled with visitors from exotic lands such as Arabia, Rhodes (an island off the coast of Greece), and Egypt.

Rowdy crowds lined the streets to watch as the procession began, led by lictors, or officers who assisted top government administrators and accompanied them on public appearances. Lictors marched in robes and carried fasces (several rods bound together with ribbon), ceremonial symbols of their authority. Next came a large group of young boys, all from good families and especially chosen by Titus to show off the youth of Rome to the foreign visitors. This group was followed by charioteers and athletes. Convicts also walked in the procession, bound together by ropes around their necks. Each wore a placard stating what his crime had been. The convicts would later be executed in the arena.

Then came the stars of the festival, the gladiators. Some gladiators carried shields and swords. Some carried daggers, and some carried spears and nets. Some wore armor or elaborately designed helmets. They were all strong and fierce. Every gladiator in the inaugural procession had already killed many men and numbered among the best gladiators the empire had to offer. They marched to the amphitheater with mechanical precision, looking neither right nor left as the crowds cheered them on.

The gladiators were followed by elephants. Ever since the general Julius Caesar had brought elephants back from Africa, all Roman processions featured the gigantic beasts. The Romans loved watching them. Wild animals in cages followed, as well as gazelles and cheetahs on leashes. Dancers came next, playing musical instruments as they wound through the streets. The smell of burning incense filled the air as the Roman priests approached, carrying statues of Roman gods. Pipes played and young girls scattered flowers across the path of the procession.

Many Romans saw elephants for the first time during the Punic Wars (264–146 B.C.). Their opponents, the Carthaginians from northern Africa, used elephants in battle.

By this time, the procession had been going on for hours and was reaching its climax—the appearance of Titus. As he came into view, the crowd broke into deafening applause, shouting out wishes for a long life. Attendants carried him on a litter (a carrying device somewhat like a chair on top of a stretcher) into the amphitheater. As Titus mounted the podium and greeted the crowd of fifty thousand, a thunderous roar filled the air. He raised his hands for silence. Then he ordered the games to begin.

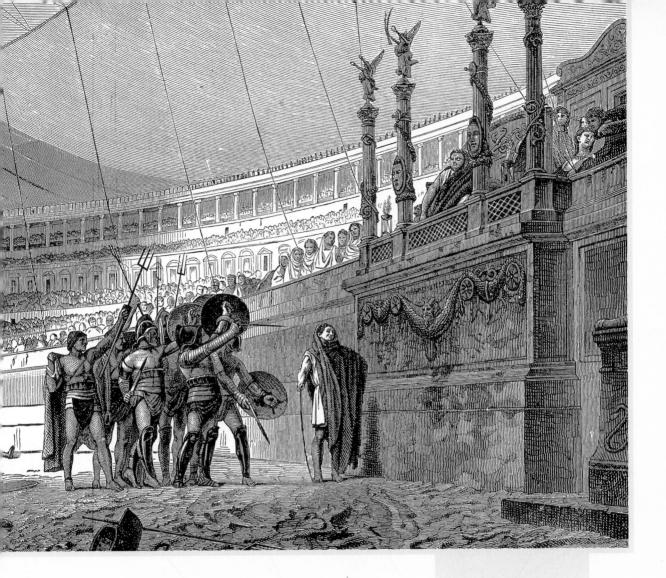

THE ORIGIN OF GLADIATOR GAMES

Gladiator games were actually fights—two armed gladiators battling until one was killed or pardoned. To be pardoned meant to be allowed to live. The tradition of gladiator games began with the Etruscans, an ancient people who occupied present-day Italy. Historians think the Etruscans believed the soul of a dead person needed to be honored by the spilling of human blood. To do this, two professional fighters were hired to fight on the grave of the departed person until one of them was killed. Only through this ritual spilling of human blood would the departed person find peace in the afterlife.

Contestants salute the Roman emperor from the arena before the day's gladiator contests start. These games evolved from an ancient Etruscan ritual.

Historical evidence suggests that the Romans had revived this ancient practice by 264 B.C., when three pairs of gladiators fought to the death at the funeral of Decimus Brutus Pera. Arranged by his sorrowing sons, the fights were a novelty that the funeralgoers found oddly compelling. Gladiator fights at funerals gradually caught on among wealthy Romans. Unlike the Etruscan fights, though, the Roman fights didn't have much to do with appeasing a dead spirit. They were more about giving the gathered crowd a good time. In addition to featuring gladiator fights, these early Roman funerals also featured banquets and theatrical performances.

As gladiator games grew in popularity, and the gladiators became more professional, the Romans dropped the pretext that the games were a funeral ritual. A wealthy Roman still might say that he was staging gladiator games to honor a dead relative, but more and more frequently the games were simply staged for what they were—a display of wealth and entertainment for the masses.

FORUMS AND CIRCUSES

Gladiator games became so popular that rulers and town officials began sponsoring them as a way to win public approval. Julius Caesar liked to sponsor gladiator games and even maintained his own troupe of five thousand gladiators.

The earliest arenas were simply open spaces surrounded by a wooden fence. The gladiators fought on a wooden platform in the middle. By approximately 90 B.C., gladiator games were being staged in circuses (elongated arenas with a spine down the middle, designed for chariot racing) and forums (open gathering places in the center of a town, often with a monument or water fountain in the middle).

When a gladiator game was held in a circus, people in the audience had a comfortable place to sit but a poor view of the event. Because circuses were really racetracks, they were long and narrow. Anyone unfortunate enough to be at one end during a gladiator game staged in a circus didn't get to see much of anything—he was too far away.

A gladiator game staged in a forum wasn't much better. The ground was flat, so only people in the first few rows could see anything. Others had to peer over the heads of the people in front of them.

Staging the games in forums presented another problem, too. As gladiator games became more elaborate, some included fights with wild animals.

THE CIRCUS MAXIMUS

The Circus Maximus *(above)* was the first and largest circus, or chariot racing arena, built by the Romans. It existed at least as early as the fourth century B.C. and was repeatedly rebuilt and refurbished. It was one of the largest structures in ancient Rome, and it could hold up to 250,000 people.

Chariots usually had two wheels and were pulled by four horses. Occasionally, dogs, ostriches, or camels were used to pull the chariots. The charioteers, or chariot drivers, wore helmets and wrapped themselves tightly in the long reins. This helped them control the horses, as well as stay more securely in the chariot. Charioteers also carried knives to cut themselves free, in case they overturned. Accidents frequently caused injuries and deaths. Four to twelve chariots raced at a time, and the course usually consisted of seven laps around the arena.

Admission to the Circus Maximus was free, and all levels of Roman society, from the emperor to the poorest laborer, came to see the chariot races. Like gladiator games, chariot races were very popular with the Roman people, and the Circus Maximus was usually packed. Inside the gates of the Circus Maximus were booths and food stalls where merchants sold food and other items. The Circus Maximus no longer exists, but the site the structure occupied can still be seen in Rome.

These games had to be staged where the animals could be confined and controlled.

THE DEVELOPMENT OF THE AMPHITHEATER

The amphitheater was a new architectural development. It was a response to a specific problem: how to seat a large number of people in a way that let them see everything that was going on.

The ancient Greeks had built theaters with raised tiers of seats, but these structures were roughly semicircular and didn't surround the action. Roman architects borrowed the Greek theater concept and extended it completely around the center of interest. The word *amphitheater* comes from two Greek words that mean "theater in the round."

The first amphitheaters were built of wood and did not stand for long. Some of them were disassembled as soon as the games held in them were finished. Others stood for several seasons before being torn down to make way for houses, temples, or other structures.

For all their popularity, gladiator games weren't staged very frequently until approximately 40 B.C. The shows were expensive to put on, and only the wealthiest individuals, such as emperors and public officials, could afford to stage them. In addition to having to pay the gladiators themselves and maintain living arrangements for them, the organizer had to construct or rent an arena. Because the games were staged so infrequently, wooden arenas were adequate for many years.

The first permanent amphitheater known to historians was constructed of stone and built in 80 B.C. in Pompeii. The city is 140 miles

> The amphitheater was a new architectural development. It was a response to a specific problem: how to seat a large number of people in a way that let them see everything that was going on. . . . The word *amphitheater* comes from two Greek words that mean "theater in the round."

(225 kilometers) southeast of Rome, on the Bay of Naples. It was buried in dense, protective ash 159 years later (A.D. 79) when a nearby volcano, Mount Vesuvius, erupted. Along with the many buildings and objects found at Pompeii, its amphitheater is well preserved. Historians have been able to learn many things about life in the Roman Empire from Pompeii.

Two prominent public officials, Valgus and Porcius, paid for Pompeii's amphitheater. An inscription dedicating the building to them can still be seen carved in stone. Because the word *amphitheater* was not yet in use, the inscription calls the structure as a *spectacula,* or a "place for spectacles."

Remains of the amphitheater in Pompeii, Italy

Rome was the capital city of the Roman Empire. It had temples, a large forum, public bathhouses, and a population of nearly one million people. Its citizens loved gladiator games, yet the city didn't get its first amphitheater until 29 B.C., a full fifty years after the amphitheater at Pompeii had been erected. It was built by Titus Statilius Taurus, a general in the army of the first Roman emperor, Augustus (who reigned from 27 B.C. to A.D. 14). It stood on the Campus Martius, a large open

TENS OF THOUSANDS KILLED IN AMPHITHEATER COLLAPSE

As gladiator games gained in popularity, many promoters sponsored the fights as a way to make money. By charging admission, they could pay for the construction of an amphitheater, pay and maintain the gladiators, and still make money. Most promoters were scrupulous, investing enough money to make their amphitheaters safe, but some were not.

In A.D. 27, an ex-slave named Atilius decided to go into the business of promoting gladiator fights. He constructed a wooden amphitheater in Fidenae, a town just north of Rome. But he didn't dig the foundation in solid ground, used poor-quality lumber, and didn't bolt the seating together properly.

Most of the town's population packed into the amphitheater to watch the opening gladiator games. Unable to bear the weight, the structure collapsed. According to an account by Tacitus, a historian writing at the end of the century, more than fifty thousand people were injured or killed.

"Those who were crushed to death in the first moment of the accident had at least under such dreadful circumstances the advantage of escaping torture," Tacitus wrote. "More to be pitied were they who with limbs torn from them still retained life, while they recognised their wives and children by seeing them during the day and by hearing in the night their screams and groans. Soon all the neighbours in their excitement at the report were bewailing brothers, kinsmen or parents. Even those whose friends or relatives were away from home for quite a different reason, still trembled for them, and as it was not yet known who had been destroyed by the crash, suspense made the alarm more widespread."

area that held many of Rome's grandest buildings. Historians don't know how large this arena was, but perhaps it wasn't large enough. In A.D. 57 Nero, the fifth Roman emperor, built a second wooden amphitheater.

THE EMPEROR NERO

Nero (who reigned from A.D. 54 to 68) was the great-great grandson of Augustus, the first Roman emperor. Nero considered himself a great artist and a sensitive poet. He used the gladiator games as a way to stage lavish shows, which sometimes featured himself reading his poems or singing his songs. Often, he accompanied his singing by playing the lyre, or small harp. Nero considered delight in a gladiator's death to be uncivilized, and he wanted no part of it. For him, the show was important, not the killing. When he held gladiator games to celebrate his crowning as emperor, he decreed that the gladiators couldn't kill each other—an order that annoyed the citizens of Rome.

During Nero's reign, gladiator shows became fantastic productions, complete with magical fountains, castles, even a lake filled with exotic sea creatures. During one show, the setting was a woodland scene of glittering bushes, sparkling waterfalls, and wild beasts.

Nero's gladiator shows were outrageously expensive. As a result, he nearly emptied the Roman treasury during his reign. The Roman government suffered because Nero was more

Emperor Nero staged such extravagant shows that he nearly emptied the Roman treasury.

interested in planning shows, writing poetry, and acting in plays than in overseeing the affairs of state.

THE HATED GOLDEN HOUSE

In A.D. 64 a fire started in the wooden seats of the Circus Maximus. For six days the fire roared through Rome, consuming everything in its path, including both of Rome's existing amphitheaters. When the fire was finally extinguished, most of the city was little more than charred, smoking rubble. Thousands of people were homeless.

After the fire, Nero established some relief programs for the homeless and began rebuilding some of the public buildings that had been destroyed. But he also claimed some of the choicest property in the city for himself, even though it had previously belonged to others. On this land, he built the Golden House, an enormous pleasure palace surrounded by a fantasy landscape. This infuriated many people, especially those who had lost land to Nero. Some came to believe Nero himself had set the fire. Some even claimed that he had stood by singing and playing the lyre as the city burned. As for Nero, he blamed the Christians. They followed a new religion, worshiping a single god and following the teachings of Jesus. As punishment for straying from the established religion, Nero had Christians tied to stakes in the garden at one of his villas and covered with flammable resin. Then he used them as torches to light the garden at night.

The Golden House was right in the center of Rome. The palace complex included an artificial lake. Along its shoreline were buildings constructed to look like miniature cities. The landscaping also included plowed fields, orderly vineyards, lush woodlands, and pastures where wild and domestic beasts roamed. The entrance hall of the Golden House contained a 120-foot (37-meter) statue of Nero, which became known as the Colossus of Nero. Much of the house was decorated with gold, and portions were studded

> "At last,
> I can live as befits
> a human being!"
> —**Nero**

with jewels and mother-of-pearl. At least one room he used for entertaining is said to have had an ivory ceiling that slid back to allow a shower of perfume to mist down on guests. When the house was completed (probably around A.D. 67), Nero arrogantly remarked, "At last, I can live as befits a human being!"

Workers at one of Nero's villas set Christians aflame *(upper right)* to light the lawn.

But the Romans still remembered Augustus, the first Roman emperor. Augustus had built lavishly for the city of Rome, yet he lived very simply himself. Nero's extravagant behavior angered many people.

The Roman army was particularly angry with Nero, because he ignored military matters and failed to earn military glory. In A.D. 68, the army proclaimed one of its own, General Galba, as its new emperor. Shortly after, the Roman Senate affirmed Galba as the next emperor and declared Nero an enemy of the people. Rather than face execution (which is how the Romans often disposed of emperors they didn't care for), Nero committed suicide. His last words were "What an artist perishes in me!"

Chapter Two
A Gift to the People

(A.D. 68–75)

NERO'S DEATH IN A.D. 68 marked the beginning of what historians refer to as the "Year of the Four Emperors." Starting with Nero, three more emperors met violent deaths that year, one after another. After Nero came General Galba, who had captured public support largely because of gladiator games he had sponsored. Roman citizens seemed unconcerned about his qualifications to be emperor. They talked more about a troupe of tightrope-walking elephants that had performed at his gladiator games.

But after becoming emperor, Galba made the mistake of refusing to pay bonuses (extra money) to the soldiers who had helped him gain power. He also selected ineffective and corrupt people to work for him, further diminishing his popularity among the Senate and the military. After Galba refused to pay soldiers who helped him on another occasion, he lost the remaining support he had. A group of soldiers, apparently unimpressed with tightrope-walking elephants, stabbed him to death in public.

The next emperor was Otho. He reigned only briefly before he was overthrown and killed. Vitellius succeeded him. Throughout this year of turmoil, Roman citizens showed little interest in who would become the next emperor, their supreme ruler. Tacitus, a philosopher and historian who wrote during that time, complained about the Romans' growing enchantment with gladiator games and their brutish indifference toward political affairs.

Above, Otho was emperor for about four months. *Opposite,* Vespasian's likeness on a Roman coin. Roman law made it treasonous (criminal) to say or do something insulting or inappropriate in the presence of the emperor himself or even in the presence of his image.

AN EMPEROR FOR THE PEOPLE

While violence and political unrest kept Rome in turmoil, a powerful general named Titus Flavius Sabinus Vespasianus, or Vespasian, was defending the empire against an uprising in the eastern province of Judea (in present-day Israel). Sure and steady, Vespasian was winning the so-called Jewish War. He was also gaining support from other powerful military figures, who saw him as an intelligent and proven leader. They wanted him to become the emperor of the Roman Empire.

Vespasian was balding but looked distinguished, with a strong brow and firm-set mouth. Although he was sixty years old in A.D. 69, his body was sturdy and healthy. He was a widower with two sons—Titus and Domitian—and a daughter who had died. Vespasian was born to the equestrian class, a class of landowners that was lower than senators but higher than regular citizens. He was born in the countryside north of Rome. His father had been a tax collector, and Vespasian grew up knowing the value of money and how to earn it. He was a compassionate man who never held grudges and possessed a great sense of humor, traits not often associated with Roman emperors. He was also shrewd, practical, and tough.

Toward the end of the Year of the Four Emperors, even as Vitellius was still settling into his role as emperor,

Vespasian was declared the new emperor by the armies of the eastern provinces. Troops supporting Vespasian descended on Italy and defeated Vitellius's troops. On December 20, A.D. 69, they killed Vitellius and proclaimed Vespasian emperor. Vespasian left the job of finishing the Jewish War to his oldest son, Titus, and spent the winter in Alexandria, Egypt. He sailed across the Mediterranean Sea and arrived in Rome in October A.D. 70.

REBUILDING ROME

Ineffective and wasteful government during the Year of the Four Emperors had left the Roman treasury nearly drained. So one of Vespasian's first concerns as emperor was to restore the treasury. He found many ingenious ways to do that, some not entirely scrupulous. He revived taxes other emperors had abolished and sold public positions to the highest bidder. He bought all the supplies of several items, then resold them at inflated prices. Rome was soon prosperous again.

Many of Vespasian's measures were met with anger at first, but he eventually managed to endear himself to the people of Rome. The money Vespasian collected went into the Roman treasury, not his own pocket. He also gave money to impoverished citizens, granted generous awards to artists and musicians, and held large public banquets. Within one year, Vespasian had become a very popular emperor.

TOILET TAXES

Vespasian inherited a government with almost no money. Nero had spent extravagantly. For one private banquet, he had spent the modern equivalent of hundreds of thousands of dollars just on roses. His successors were no more frugal. So when it came to collecting taxes and replenishing funds, Vespasian was willing to try almost anything. He even levied a tax on the public toilets of Rome.

His oldest son, Titus, was embarrassed by the tax. No other Roman emperor had taxed public toilets. But when Titus complained to his father, Vespasian held out a coin to him and said, "See, my son, if it has any smell." As far as Vespasian was concerned, money was money, no matter where it came from.

Vespasian was determined to erase all traces of Nero and to be a true leader for the people of Rome. The enormous statue of Nero still stood outside the Golden House, but Vespasian ordered the head resculpted into the likeness of Apollo, the Roman god of sunlight, prophecy, music, and poetry. The statue eventually came to be known simply as the Colossus.

Vespasian also did other, more important things to make people forget about Nero. Nero had used the fire of 64 that had consumed much of Rome as an excuse to take land away from people. In contrast, Vespasian started a huge construction program to rebuild the city and give land back to those who had lost it. To inaugurate the rebuilding of the downtown area, Vespasian personally collected the first basket of rubble and carried it away on his shoulders. Almost simultaneously he started work on two new

Slaves, such as those building a Roman road in this relief, or type of sculpture, did most of the menial work in ancient Rome.

temples and a forum. He also authorized people to claim vacant land if the original owners could not be found.

Roman citizens appreciated temples and forums, but any emperor who wanted to stay in power also needed to provide entertainment for the people. Gladiator games were one of the most popular forms of entertainment. But to hold gladiator games, Rome would need an amphitheater. What better gift from a benevolent, popular emperor than the most magnificent amphitheater on earth?

Vespasian *(seated)* studies an architect's model for a grand amphitheater.

THE AMPHITHEATER IN THE LAKE

Building an amphitheater as large as the one Vespasian imagined would require a lot of space. Vespasian must have met with the building's architect, or with a team of architects, to discuss a suitable location. As it turned out, Vespasian's plans for a permanent amphitheater meshed perfectly with his desire to erase all traces of Nero. Nero's personal estate provided an ideal place for the amphitheater.

The site of the Golden House was certainly large enough for an amphitheater. But it could not be used until the house was torn down. Because Nero was so despised, the house was being dismantled anyway and its materials used for other projects. But the huge task of demolition was proceeding slowly, and in the early 70s the house was still largely standing.

Vespasian and his architect decided to use the land under Nero's artificial lake as the site for the new amphitheater. Using the lake bed would eliminate the need to tear down the Golden House immediately. The obvious problem with this site, though, was getting the water out of the lake.

To drain the lake, workmen dug deep trenches between the lake and the nearby Tiber River. They lined the trenches with blocks of stone, covered them with tiles, and then buried them. Water from the lake then flowed through the trenches into the river.

This underground drainage system, installed before construction on the amphitheater even began, is one of the reasons why so much of the building is still standing, nearly two thousand years after its construction. As soon as rain sinks into the ground, it encounters the sewer system and drains away. This continual drainage has kept the site dry and the foundation stable. Without adequate drainage, the site would have become waterlogged and the building might have settled and sunk, causing cracks in the structure.

THE DESIGN

The Golden House and other buildings Nero constructed during his reign were largely experimental, and many people considered them strange. But Vespasian was a conservative person who wanted no part of Nero's radical architecture. He was more concerned that his building meet two important architectual challenges: safely supporting its immense weight

The tiered seating in modern football stadiums, such as this one in Baltimore, Maryland, resembles the seating in the Flavian Amphitheater.

and making it easy for fifty thousand people to use. Vespasian's building was going to be large, solid, and functional—like Vespasian himself.

The Flavian Amphitheater would be an enormous oval, 620 feet (189 m) long by 513 feet (156 m) wide. The facade, or exterior wall, would rise more than 156 feet (48 m) high—higher than a modern fifteen-story apartment building.

In the center of the building would be the arena floor—the staging area for gladiator fights and other spectacles. It would be a smaller oval, 287 feet (87 m) by 180 feet (55 m). Tiers of seats would rise around it from the floor to the top of the exterior wall, similar to the seating in a modern football stadium.

The *cavea,* or seating area, would rest on a skeleton of giant piers, or pillars, of travertine (a hard form of limestone). The piers would be arranged in seven rings of eighty piers each. Looking out from inside the arena, the piers would radiate outward in eighty rows, like the spokes of a wheel. Each row would be made up of seven piers (one from each ring).

Giant stones of tufa (a kind of volcanic rock) would fill the spaces between the middle piers of each row, forming walls. These are called radial walls, because they radiate out from the center.

Aerial View of Colosseum Structural Support Skeleton

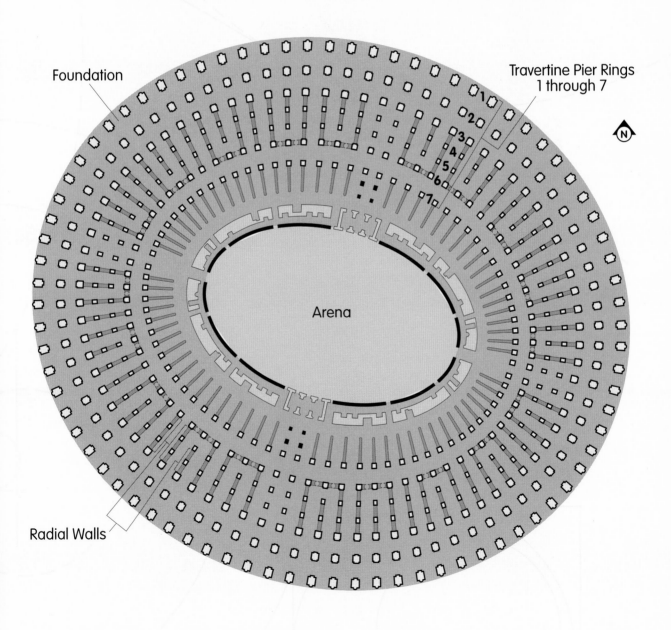

Barrel Vault

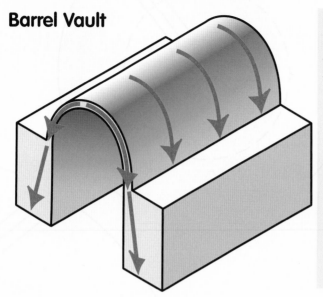

Barrel vaults shift the weight from the ceiling to the side walls.

Near the arena floor, the radial walls would need to be only about 15 feet (4.5 m) high to support the lowest rows of seats. But toward the exterior wall, they would have to reach much higher to support the highest seats in the back rows. In the spaces between the eighty radial walls the architect specified eighty radial walkways and staircases. The outside ends of the walkways would function as entrances to the building. Concrete barrel vaults would cover these walkways, connecting the radial walls to each other and allowing seats and more walkways and staircases to be built on top of them. A barrel vault is a long, tunnel-shaped ceiling over a corridor. A barrel vault transfers weight away from the middle of the ceiling into the haunches, or side walls, of the vault. For this reason, a vaulted ceiling does not need to be supported in the middle. The haunches contain the travertine piers and are strong enough to support all the weight. Barrel vaults are an important feature of the amphitheater because they transfer the weight of the building onto the sturdy travertine piers.

An elaborate design had been created for the amphitheater, one that would produce a sturdy and easy-to-use building. The site had been identified and drained. The building also gained its name. It would be called the Flavian Amphitheater, after Vespasian's family name. It was time to start construction on the largest amphitheater the Romans had ever seen.

EIGHTY ENTRANCES

The eighty radial walls in the Flavian Amphitheater created eighty radial corridors to be used as entrances. But only seventy-six entrances were for use by the public. The four other entrances (one each on the north, south, east, and west sides of the building) were not for public use. The emperor and his guests used the south entrance. High-ranking officials and the Vestal Virgins (the only female priests of Rome) used the north entrance. Through the west entrance gladiators, musicians, and other players entered the arena. The east entrance was the so-called "gate of death," where the gladiators exited, dead or alive.

Vestal Virgins *(below)* served at the Temple of Vesta in Rome for a term of thirty years—ten as students, ten in direct service to Vesta, and ten as teachers.

Chapter Three

THE FOUNDATION AND LOWER LEVEL

(A.D. 75–77)

THE FLAVIAN AMPHITHEATER was going to be huge and heavy. Constructed almost entirely of stone and concrete, it would need a massive foundation to keep it from shifting or sinking into the ground.

The foundation would be a circular concrete trench that was 40 feet (12 m) deep and shaped like a doughnut. The cavea would rest on it. The depression of the lake bed was already about 20 feet (6 m) deep. So work crews had to dig only about 20 feet (6 m) deeper. They loaded the excavated dirt into ox-drawn carts that hauled it to the outskirts of town. Historians estimate that 33,000 tons (30,000 metric tons) of earth were probably removed from the site.

Legend has it that twenty thousand to thirty thousand semiskilled and unskilled workers built the Flavian Amphitheater.

Once the trench was excavated, concrete was poured into it in layers. After each layer dried, another was added. The lowest layers were poured directly into the clay subsoil, which could easily retain the concrete. Closer to the surface, the earth was not as strong as the clay subsoil, so workers lined the sides of the trench with brick walls, then poured concrete between them.

On top of the concrete foundation, workers laid three layers of travertine blocks. Each layer was about 3 feet (1 m) thick. The top layer would be the bottom floor of the amphitheater. Some of the stones became the bases of the mighty travertine piers. The Flavian Amphitheater would

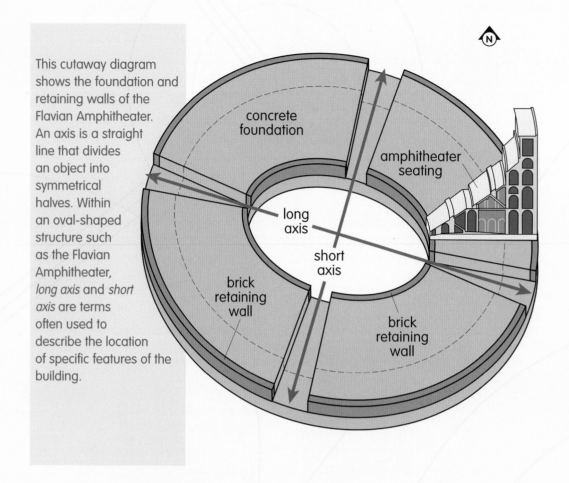

This cutaway diagram shows the foundation and retaining walls of the Flavian Amphitheater. An axis is a straight line that divides an object into symmetrical halves. Within an oval-shaped structure such as the Flavian Amphitheater, *long axis* and *short axis* are terms often used to describe the location of specific features of the building.

concrete foundation

amphitheater seating

long axis

short axis

brick retaining wall

brick retaining wall

have many toilets and fountains, so a network of drainpipes was laid between the layers of stones. These led to additional pipes under the stones, which drained into the city's sewer system. A small forest of short pipes probably protruded from the top of the stone layers, just waiting to be hooked up to pipes that would be installed in the amphitheater's walls. These would carry water throughout the building.

TRAVERTINE AND CRANES

The travertine used in the floor and support piers was painstakingly carved from quarries near the town of Tivoli, about 25 miles (40 km) away from the amphitheater. Operating without the benefit of explosives or machines, workers cut blocks of travertine from the earth with saws. Historians estimate that 3.5 million cubic feet (110,000 cubic m) of travertine was used in the Flavian Amphitheater. On average each block in the piers weighed about 4.5 tons (4 metric tons).

After each block was pulled from the quarry, highly skilled stone-cutters shaped it by hand. They used saws and sand to wear away the stone to the dimensions given by the architect.

Next the blocks were loaded onto carts and pulled by teams of oxen to Rome. They were probably unloaded in the center of the amphitheater—the arena. Since no work had been done on the arena yet, it was simply an empty space perfect for use as a workyard and storage area for materials. Once the blocks arrived at the site, they were carefully shaped by artisans, using hammers and chisels, to fit a specific spot. When needed, the enormous blocks were hoisted into place with mechanical cranes, powered by workers and teams of animals. The A-frame crane was probably used at both the quarry and the construction site. These A-frame cranes could lift to a height of about 40 feet (13 m).

An A-frame crane works together with a rope-and-pulley system. The crane consists of two legs (beams of wood) lashed together at the top and spread apart at the bottom. This shape looks like an "A."

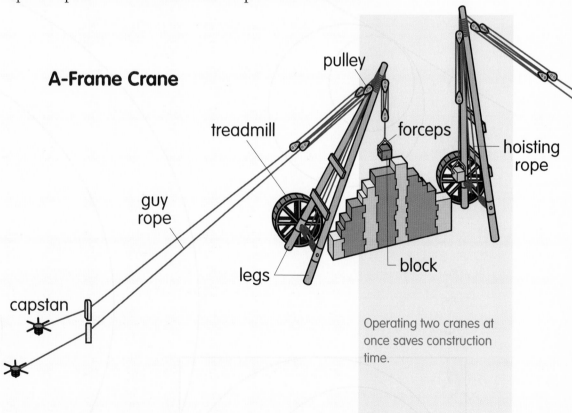

A-Frame Crane

pulley

treadmill

forceps

hoisting rope

guy rope

legs

block

capstan

Operating two cranes at once saves construction time.

The capstans used in constructing the amphitheater were similar to the screw press *(above)* used at the time for making wine. To turn the press or capstan, workers or animals walked in a circle pushing big spokes extending from the center.

A rope, called the guy rope, is attached to the top of the legs. It runs away from the crane and attaches to a wheel called a capstan. The capstan is anchored firmly into the ground and turns (like a merry-go-round). As it turns one way, it winds the guy rope more tightly. This raises the top of the crane. As the capstan turns the other way, it lets out the guy rope. This lowers the top of the crane.

At the top of the crane is a pulley. Looped over the pulley is another rope, called the hoisting rope, which lifts the block. Rope-and-pulley systems can help workers hoist many more pounds than they could lift with just their arms.

At the Flavian Amphitheater, workers positioned each crane near the end of a radial wall. One end of the hoisting rope was attached to a set of giant forceps (like ice tongs). A stone block was hauled in front of the crane. Then workers clamped the forceps to the block.

At the bottom of the crane, at the other end of the hoisting rope, was a giant hollow wheel called a treadmill. The treadmill was more than 10 feet (3 m) high inside. Workers or animals walked inside it, like hamsters in an exercise wheel. As they turned the treadmill, it reeled in the hoisting rope. As the rope tightened, it lifted the block of stone.

Once the stone had been lifted, workers or animals turned the capstan, letting out the guy rope and lowering the crane's legs. This moved the top of the crane—and the stone—forward, toward the wall. When the stone was above the spot where it was needed, the treadmill was turned to lower the stone into place. Workers used levers to rock each block into perfect position next to the others. If a block didn't fit well, it was recut by one of the expert stonecutters at the site.

Once in place, the large blocks were bonded together with iron clamps. Working with iron was a specialized skill. Blacksmiths, ironworkers, and

The treadmill *(lower left)*, shown in this relief from the tomb of an ancient Roman family, is similar to those used in constructing the Flavian Amphitheater. Workers or animals march along inside the treadmill, providing power to operate ropes and pulleys that hoist the load.

bronze workers were needed for this phase of construction. Thousands of clamps were used. Most were probably made in off-site blacksmith forges and delivered as part of the supplies. But there was probably a blacksmith at the construction site to handle repairs and precise alterations. About 300 tons (270 metric tons) of iron were used in Level 1 alone to keep stones in place. Molten lead was also poured into the clamp holes to keep the clamps from shifting and to protect the iron from rusting.

Ancient Roman blacksmiths shaped iron into sophisticated household fixtures, such as locks and hinges.

BUILDING UP THE WALLS

For purposes of identification, people who study the Colosseum have assigned numbers to each ring of travertine piers. Pier Ring 1 refers to the tallest, outermost ring of piers that are part of the facade. Pier Ring 2 is the next ring in, and so on, with Pier Ring 7 referring to the shortest ring of piers closest to the arena floor. The two rings of piers closest to the exterior wall (Pier Rings 1 and 2) would be freestanding, with no walls between them, allowing people to walk through circular walkways. The space between Pier Rings 6 and 7 (the rings of piers closest to the arena floor) would also be freestanding, creating another circular walkway next to the arena. The spaces between Pier Rings 3 to 6 would be filled with blocks of tufa, creating the radial support walls.

After the floor stones were laid, workers probably began laying the travertine stones for the middle piers, Pier Rings 3 to 6. By starting in the middle and working outward, the workers could have cranes operating simultaneously on both the inside (arena side) and the outside (facade side) of the cavea. Separate crews probably worked on several of the eighty radial walls at the same time.

The crews probably placed the travertine stone for the piers and the tufa "filling" stones at the same time. It would have been easier to lay both kinds of stone at the same time rather than trying to wedge the tufa filling stones in between the already standing piers. The two types of stone were fitted together like a jigsaw puzzle and built as a single wall. The travertine piers are still visible, sandwiched between walls of tufa.

Interlocked layers of travertine and tufa blocks are clearly visible in this exterior view of Levels 2 and 3.

Construction of Level 1

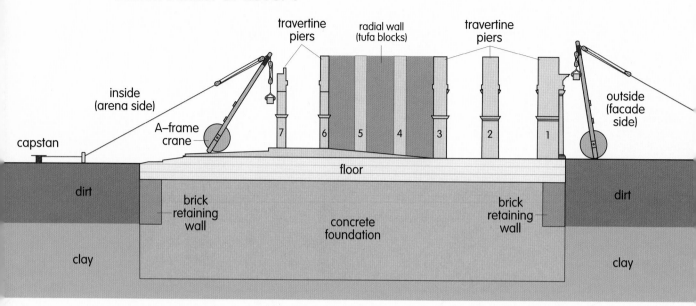

As the radial walls went higher, another crew of workers installed water pipes in recesses already cut into the piers. Then they connected the pipes to the water pipes that had been previously laid in the foundation.

Once a radial wall had reached the full height of Level 1, both cranes—the one on the arena side and the one on the facade side— began work on Pier Rings 1, 2, and 7. The inside crane built Pier Ring 7, while the outside crane built Pier Ring 2 and then Pier Ring 1. At their full height, piers in Pier Ring 7 would be only about 15 feet (4.5 m) high, since they would support only the lowest rows of seats in the cavea. The piers in Pier Rings 1 and 2 would eventually reach the top of Level 3, but at this point in construction they were probably only built up to the top of Level 1.

BARREL VAULTS

When all the stonework of Level 1 was finished, the radial corridors (between the radial walls) and circular corridors (which circled the building between Pier Rings 6 and 7, 1 and 2, and 2 and 3) had to be roofed over with barrel vaults. Vaulting specialists built the barrel vaults. The cranes were moved out of the way to make room for the vaulting crew. Their first step was to build scaffolding (a framework that attaches to a building and has platforms for workers to stand on). Standing on the scaffolding, the vaulting crews constructed wooden, vault-shaped forms on top of the walls. Next the crews poured concrete into the vault-shaped forms. After the concrete hardened, the wooden forms were removed, leaving behind concrete vaults. On top of the vaults the concrete was flat, becoming the floor of Level 2.

About sixty of the eighty radial corridors became a stairwell. The barrel vaults over these corridors did not cover the entire corridor—the vaulting crews left open spaces where the stairs led to Level 2. Other workers constructed the stairways.

Barrel vaults functioned both as corridor ceilings and as supports for the floors of the next level in the Flavian Amphitheater.

Chapter Four
THE UPPER LEVELS AND FINISHING WORK

(A.D. 77–79)

VESPASIAN WAS A BUSY MAN. He spent most of his life in the military, traveling throughout the empire. During the earlier reign of Claudius (41–54), Vespasian oversaw the Roman expansion into Great Britain. At the time of Vespasian's proclamation as emperor, he was in Judea, commanding sixty thousand men in the Jewish War. He had been governor of Judea and of Africa.

Yet after Vespasian became emperor, he stayed in Rome, often sending his

The Flavian Amphitheater was Vespasian's largest building project.

oldest son, Titus, to oversee military operations abroad. His habit of being busy didn't change, though. He merely transferred his energy to restoring and managing the empire. Building projects were an important part of this job.

Vespasian visited all of his building projects in Rome regularly. He probably visited the amphitheater site frequently, perhaps in the company of one of his sons, urging the workers along. The amphitheater was his gift to the people, and he wanted it finished as soon as possible.

Vespasian would have had another reason for hurrying the project along. He was in his mid-sixties, already old by the standards of the time. The Flavian Amphitheater was his masterpiece, the grandest thing Rome had ever seen. He wanted it finished and dedicated before he died.

Construction of Level 2

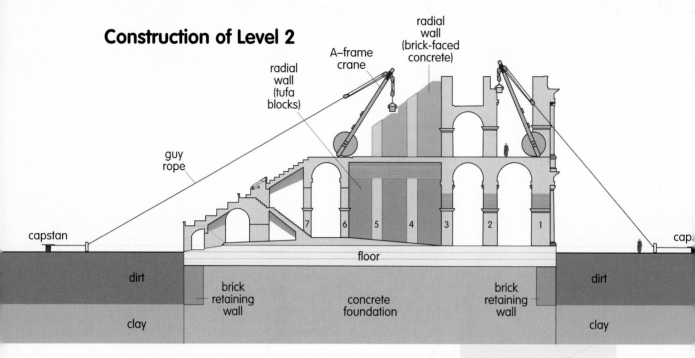

radial
wall
(brick-faced
concrete)

A–frame
crane

radial
wall
(tufa
blocks)

guy
rope

capstan

cap.

7 6 5 4 3 2 1

floor

dirt

brick
retaining
wall

concrete
foundation

brick
retaining
wall

dirt

clay

clay

THE PIERS AND RADIAL WALLS

Construction on Level 2 of the amphitheater may have begun around A.D. 77. Cranes were again needed to lift the massive travertine blocks of the piers for Level 2. The cranes may have been carried by hand or lifted by other cranes to get them up to Level 2. The capstans still had to be anchored in the ground and were cranked on the ground.

Like the travertine piers, the filling between the piers was also extended upward. But unlike on Level 1, the filling was made of brick-faced concrete instead of blocks of tufa. Workers carried concrete and bricks in baskets up the stairs. For this level, they built the piers to full height instead of laying one layer at a time, as they had on Level 1. Then between the piers they built two parallel brick walls, the faces of the radial walls. They filled the space between the brick walls with concrete, the core of the radial walls.

Construction materials changed because concrete and brick are lighter than tufa. It was important to reduce the weight of Level 2. Concrete and brick are also weaker than tufa. But the radial walls this high up did not need to be as strong as the walls on Level 1 because they wouldn't be holding up as much weight.

The proportions of the Flavian Amphitheater must have awed the workers building it.

Although the work with concrete and brick on Level 2 may have been easier than the work with tufa blocks on Level 1, conditions on Level 2 were more hazardous. The working surface was much smaller than on Level 1. The floor ended with a drop-off at Pier Ring 1 and only extended inward to Pier Ring 5. Between Pier Rings 5 and 7, the floor sloped down sharply to the place where the lowest rows of seats would eventually appear. Workers also had to watch out for the voids in the floor where the stairwells opened up.

When the piers and radial walls were finished on Level 2, the corridors between them were roofed with barrel vaults, just as they had been on Level 1. Once again, a floor was created on top of the vaults, and then construction on Level 3 began.

The floor on Level 3 had stairwell voids, just like Level 2. But here the floor was even smaller, extending only to Pier Ring 3. Still, workers carried cranes up to, or used other cranes to lift them up to, this level. Again they hoisted blocks of travertine, continuing to build up the support piers. Even at Level 4, where the floor was only as wide as the distance between Pier Rings 1 and 2, cranes were probably used to hoist blocks and columns.

WALKWAYS AND STAIRWAYS

On Level 1, the corridors created between the eighty radial walls became entrances to the building. About sixty of the eighty corridors held a stairway leading to the second floor. Stairways and corridors were formed between the radial walls on higher levels, too. Other walkways and stairways ran along the circular corridors. In all, there were eighty entrances and hundreds of stairways, allowing crowds of up to fifty thousand people to find their seats and move around the amphitheater easily.

The stairways were built along with the walls and barrel vaults for each level. This gave workers access to the next level. Although cranes hoisted the bulkiest and heaviest materials to the upper levels, workers transported all other materials by hand.

THE EXTERIOR WALL

While workers bustled about inside the amphitheater, building the radial support walls and stairways, work also progressed outside. The architects designed the facade to look massive, impressive, and beautiful.

The facade went up as each level of the interior went up. By A.D. 79 much of the exterior wall was probably already finished.

Arches adorned the facade at every level. On Level 1 the arches opened into barrel-vaulted walkways, where people could enter and exit the building. Each archway entrance was framed with half-columns. A half-column is a column that appears to have been cut in half vertically and has been sculpted out of a wall. Entrances weren't needed on Levels 2 and 3, but arches and half-columns were included anyway, giving a unified appearance to the whole building.

The columns and half-columns on each level had a different type of capital, or top. On Level 1 the columns had Doric capitals, the simplest of all capitals. On Level 2 the columns had Ionic capitals. Ionic capitals are fancier, with a scroll pattern. On Levels 3 and 4 the columns had the fanciest capitals, Corinthian. Corinthian capitals are large and feature an elaborate pattern of leaves.

Level 4 of the facade looks different from the other three levels. Rectangular (instead of rounded) half-columns, called pilasters, stretch across the facade there. Each pilaster measures 45 feet (14 m) high and is topped with a Corinthian capital. Forty rectangular windows were cut out of the alternate bays (spaces) between the pilasters.

Types of Capitals

Doric   Ionic   Corinthian

THE CAVEA

For contrast, rectangular shapes dominate the design of Level 4.

Once all four levels were up and the main stairways were in place, workers began constructing the cavea. The cavea was the last major phase of construction, and it was also the simplest part of the building. Every seat in the Flavian Amphitheater was about 23 inches (58 centimeters) wide. The standard size made installing the seats simple.

To construct the cavea, workers built more stairways up the cavea surface (to enable spectators to get into the sections of seats), then put rows of seats down, laying them out in long lines between each stairway—similar to a modern basketball or football stadium.

Spectators would be seated in the amphitheater according to their social class, and so the seats of the cavea were constructed out of different materials to reflect the different classes. The seats closest to the arena, where the most important people would sit, were white marble. Seats in the middle were probably concrete. Those in the highest levels were most likely wood.

Vespasian wanted the Flavian Amphitheater to be a gift for everyone, a place where all the people of Rome mingled, but the seating arrangements were rigid. The cavea was divided into five separate zones, called *maeniana,* and each social class (or gender) had its own assigned zone. During spectacles, attendants helped people find their seats and also kicked out anyone who tried to sit in the wrong section.

The first maenianum was the podium. Seats in the podium were the closest to the action and were reserved for the highest ranking officials in the empire and their guests. Part of the podium was the *pulvinar,* the emperor's royal box located at one end of the short axis in the amphitheater. Opposite the pulvinar was another special box for the Vestal Virgins.

The second zone of seats, called the *ima cavea,* was assigned to senators and wealthy private citizens. Higher up, in the third zone, sat Rome's middle class: merchants, tradesmen, engineers, farmers, and so on. This zone was referred to as the *media cavea.* The fourth zone, called the *summa cavea,* was for slaves and foreigners. And the fifth zone—wooden seating tucked under the Level 4 colonnade, or ring of columns—was reserved for the wives and daughters of wealthy citizens. Women had been seated farthest from the arena floor ever since Augustus declared they should be shielded from the sight of blood. This uppermost zone was referred to as the *summum maenianum in ligneis.*

Not only did the most high-ranking members of Roman society get the best seats in the amphitheater, they were also allotted far more seats. About 62 percent of the seats in the building were reserved for the emperor and his attendants and guests, senators, equestrians, and the wealthiest citizens. About 20 percent of the seats were set aside for the wives and daughters of wealthy citizens. This left about 18 percent of the building for slaves, foreigners, and poor people.

Below, a partial reconstruction of Colosseum seating in the 1930s suggests how the cavea may have looked when it was finished. *Right,* a cross section of the Colosseum cavea

DEDICATION AND DEATH

By A.D. 79 the Flavian Amphitheater was nearly finished. Vespasian was also nearly finished. According to the historian Suetonius, writing a few decades later, Vespasian caught a fever that year but insisted on carrying on with his imperial duties. His condition worsened until he was near death. Yet he wanted to dedicate the amphitheater before he died, whether the great building was finished or not.

Attendants carried the dying emperor, wrapped in blankets and lying on a stretcher, through the barely finished walkways of the building and onto the arena floor. Feebly raising his hands, Vespasian dedicated the Flavian Amphitheater to the glory of the Roman Empire.

Vespasian was determined to work hard to the end. Back at home, he struggled to rise from his bed, insisting that a Roman emperor should die on his feet. He managed to get out of bed, only to collapse in the arms of his attendants. He maintained his sense of humor, though, right up to the end. As his life faded, he looked around the room and said, "Oh dear, I think I'm becoming a god." He died on June 23, A.D. 79, at the age of sixty-nine.

A Cross Section of the Cavea

summum maenianum in ligneis

mast (awning support)

attic (roof support)

colonnade

Level 4

summa cavea

Level 3

media cavea

Level 2

radial wall (brick)

ima cavea

Level 1

podium

radial wall (tufa)

7 6 5 4 3 2 1

arena

plaza

Chapter Five
THE FLAVIAN AMPHITHEATER OPENS

(79–80)

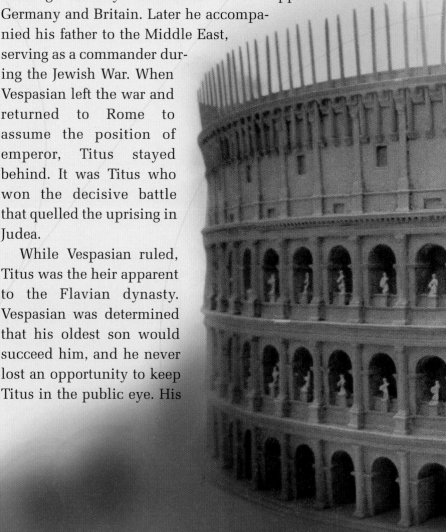

WITH VESPASIAN'S DEATH, his oldest son, Titus (who reigned from 79 to 81), inherited both the position of emperor and the job of finishing the Flavian Amphitheater. Even before his father became emperor, Titus had spent most of his life being groomed for a public position. As a boy, he attended school at the emperor's palace, studying with Nero's son, Britannicus. Titus was active in the Roman army and served as a high-ranking military official in both Upper Germany and Britain. Later he accompanied his father to the Middle East, serving as a commander during the Jewish War. When Vespasian left the war and returned to Rome to assume the position of emperor, Titus stayed behind. It was Titus who won the decisive battle that quelled the uprising in Judea.

While Vespasian ruled, Titus was the heir apparent to the Flavian dynasty. Vespasian was determined that his oldest son would succeed him, and he never lost an opportunity to keep Titus in the public eye. His

This scale model of the Flavian Amphitheater shows how it might have looked when it was finished.

efforts paid off. Upon Vespasian's death, Titus was unanimously proclaimed by the senate to be the next emperor. Titus assumed his duties in June of 79, and he took his position seriously. He poured a large amount of money into public projects and quickly developed a reputation for being kind and generous. Perhaps his greatest generosity was reserved for the Flavian Amphitheater, which had been so important to his father. Titus was eager to finish what Vespasian had begun.

LEVEL 4 AND DECORATIVE WORK

Level 4 of the amphitheater, which was the width of the distance between Pier Rings 1 and 2, was probably completed under Titus. A colonnade of 30-foot (9-m) columns was

The Roman Empire, A.D. 79

installed on this floor. The colonnade stood directly on top of Pier Ring 2. Spectators in this section would sit behind the colonnade. Behind this seating area, directly on top of Pier Ring 1, was a solid wall, called the attic. The columns and the attic served as inner and outer supports, respectively, for a continuous wooden roof that shaded the seating on Level 4.

Much of the work done under Titus was decorative. Outside, statues of gods, past emperors, and gladiators were placed in the arches of Levels 2 and 3—160 statues in all. The area around the building was paved with stone, creating a plaza that extended 57.4 feet (17.5 m) from the perimeter of the Colosseum. An enormous multi-storied fountain graced the main entrance. Inside, some walls were decorated with frescos (paintings painted directly onto wet plastered walls). White marble fountains bubbled in circular walkways on every level of the building but the fourth. Purple paint covered the vaulted ceilings above the public stairways.

One of the final jobs was to finish the arena. It was covered with fine sand to absorb blood and keep the combatants from slipping. At the end of each day's spectacle, the blood-stained sand would be removed and fresh sand deposited.

Titus's brother and successor, Domitian (who reigned from 81 to 96), commissioned the Meta Sudans fountain for the amphitheater complex. Its lower tiers could still be seen in this early twentieth-century photo *(middle right)*, but they were removed for road construction in 1936. The fountain was originally 56 feet (17 m) tall, and its base was 21 feet (7 m) in diameter.

Spectacles often included wild animal fights, so audience safety was a high priority. A wall roughly 12 feet (4 m) high was erected around the arena floor and faced with marble, providing a slippery barrier. In front of the wall, large poles were driven into the arena floor, and a net was strung between them. In case any animals managed to break through the net, scale the wall, and reach the top, ivory rollers, like giant rolling pins, were installed on top of the wall. No animal would be able to get a grip because the rollers would spin under its paws. As a final measure, archers were stationed around the arena wall.

Even with the building nearly finished, hundreds of workers still scurried around the amphitheater, adding finishing touches, sweeping dust out of passageways, scrubbing paint smears and handprints off walls, and clearing out the last of the construction debris. In A.D. 80, one year after Vespasian's death, the Flavian Amphitheater was finished enough to stage its first gladiator game.

LET THE GAMES BEGIN!

Opening day was a public holiday. All of Rome turned out to watch the procession. Government officials, jugglers, horseback riders, young boys, and musicians all paraded through the streets of Rome, making their way to the amphitheater. Tame cheetahs walked on leashes and elephants made their way past throngs of onlookers. The grand finale of the procession was the emperor Titus himself.

On the large paved plaza surrounding the amphitheater, a carnival atmosphere prevailed. Vendors sold sausages and souvenirs, drinks and fruit. Petty thieves and pickpockets roamed the plaza, looking for unwary victims. Under the hot Mediterranean sun, crowds of people moved from stall to stall, eating, drinking, and shopping. Over the noise of the crowd, music could be heard as the procession neared its destination.

With the arrival of the procession, a sense of urgency filled the crowd, and people began moving toward the entrances. The Flavian Amphitheater had seventy-six public entrances and hundreds of stairways to help audience members get to their seats. Each entrance, walkway, and stairway had a number and led to a specific section of the cavea. Pottery shards, marked with the entrance number and assigned seating area, were probably used as tickets. Event tickets indicated the correct stairway to use as well as the correct seat. Tickets were usually free and highly sought after.

ROMAN SUNSCREEN

Gladiator games usually lasted all day. Spending ten hours under the fierce rays of the sun would have been very uncomfortable for spectators. So, like other amphitheaters in the empire, the Flavian Amphitheater had an enormous velarium, or awning, that stretched over it when the sun became too intense.

The velarium was pulled across the cavea during the hottest part of the day, then retracted when the sun began to sink. A system of masts, pulleys, and ropes was used to maneuver the velarium, similar to the way sails are raised and lowered on ships. One hundred sixty winches (drumlike turning devices, similar to the capstans used with cranes) were used to move the velarium back and forth across the amphitheater. The masts were slid through stone loops at the top of the building and rested in brackets on the facade. Many of these brackets are still intact. The men operating the masts for the velarium walked on the roof above the attic on Level 4. The imprints of the stairs used to access the roof can still be seen on the inside of the attic.

Specially chosen sailors from the Roman naval bases of Misenum or Ravenna operated the velarium. At least 640 sailors were needed—four to eight men to operate each winch. For every gladiator game, manipulating the velarium required as many as one thousand sailors to be on hand. It was probably an honor to be chosen to operate the velarium at the Flavian Amphitheater.

Brackets for the velarium masts may still be seen on the facade above the windows of Level 4. There are three brackets between each half-column.

Above, lions were popular participants in venationes, or games pitting gladiators against animals.

THE OPENING ACT: ANIMALS

The first events of the day were games involving animals. These games, called the *venationes,* were the traditional way to open a day of gladiator games. To prepare animals for venationes, the animals were usually deprived of food and water for days before their appearance. Animals maddened by hunger and thirst attacked anything they saw. Sometimes wild animals were released in the arena and simply hunted down by trained fighters. Other venationes included special animal fights, such as a wrestling match between a human and a crocodile, or the slow killing of a massive lion whose mane had been gilded with pure gold.

"WE WHO ARE ABOUT TO DIE SALUTE YOU!"

As the venationes ended, the crowd began to get more excited. Venationes were just a warm-up for what the crowds really wanted to see—the fights between the gladiators. The gladiators entered the arena in a colorful procession. They were accompanied by jugglers, acrobats, and other entertainers. Musicians played trumpets, drums, and flutes. At the close of the procession, the entertainers exited the arena, and the gladiators approached the emperor's box. Standing in rows, they raised their weapons and soberly recited, "We who are about to die salute you!"

Gladiators were a separate class of Roman society. They became gladiators in different ways. Some gladiators were free men who willingly signed up for training. Some had once been in the Roman army

THE ANIMAL TRADE

When the venationes first started, wealthy citizens usually sponsored them. These citizens owned land in far parts of the empire and could have servants capture exotic animals and ship them to Rome. Roman generals also brought wild animals to Rome as part of the spoils of war.

With the building of the Flavian Amphitheater, though, a more organized method of obtaining animals was needed. A thriving network sprang up across the empire, solely for the capture and transport of animals, such as those featured in a Roman mosaic from about A.D. 200 (below). By imperial decree, every town in the empire was obligated to provide food and transport for beasts (and their keepers) traveling to Rome for the games. Many captured beasts were sent to the port of Ostia, where they were put in special cages and shipped to Rome.

but signed up to become gladiators after they were discharged. Other gladiators were slaves, condemned to the gladiator schools by their masters. Regardless of his previous status, once a man became a gladiator, he was bound by a set of rules separate from ordinary citizens. To learn his trade, he attended special schools, often practicing and studying fighting methods for years before entering the arena.

The Roman historian Petronius, Vespasian's contemporary, noted that each gladiator took a chilling and solemn oath *(sacramentum gladiatorium)*, "I will endure to be burned, to be bound, to be beaten and to be killed by the sword." This act of submission impressed Romans and made them view gladiators as examples of honor. The historian Cicero praised gladiators, stating, "There is nothing they put higher than giving satisfaction to their owner or to the

> ### "I will endure to be burned, to be bound, to be beaten and to be killed by the sword."
> **—Gladiator's oath, as recorded by Petronius**

people." Yet gladiators were also the licensed killers of the empire. They were trained to kill, and this fact, balanced against the honorable notion of dying for your betters, made the Romans both love and hate the gladiators.

There were at least sixteen different types of gladiators, each armed with different weapons and each trained in a different fighting method. Yet all gladiators fell loosely into one of five categories: mounted fighters, charioteers, heavily armed fighters, lightly armed fighters, and fighters armed only with nets and spears.

The mounted fighters were called *equites.* These gladiators might be armed in any fashion, but they always fought on horseback. The charioteers were called *essedarii.* Their weapons could also vary, but they always fought in chariots.

The other types of gladiators fought on the ground in hand-to-hand combat and were distinguished by their weapons and armor. The

many types of heavily armed gladiators relied on brute strength. Each type had a distinguishing helmet, shield, and other armor. The *murmillos,* for instance, were symbolic fishermen. Their heavy helmets displayed a fish-shaped crest. The *hoplomachi* had bare chests, but they wore massive helmets, and their right arms and left legs were sheathed in armor.

The lightly armed *Thraeces* had to be quick. Thraeces were equipped with short curved swords and small round shields. They dodged their opponents, looking for the opportunity to administer a death thrust.

Above, figures from the Trojan War (1200s B.C.) decorate this gladiator helmet from first century Pompeii. Historical or mythic figures and symbols on gladiatorial armor distinguish it from military armor. *Right,* gladiators got additional protection from greaves, or armored leggings, but they were awkward to wear in contests.

The *retiarii* were armed only with nets and spears, symbolic of the sea and mermen (mythic creatures who are part man and part fish). Because a retiarius had no defensive weapons, he too had to be quick. He fought by dodging his opponent until he could entangle him in his net and stab him with his spear.

The winner of a gladiator fight sometimes received prize money. The best gladiators could become wealthy. Sometimes the emperor granted freedom to a gladiator who became a favorite of the crowd. But wealth and freedom were not achieved very frequently.

THE GLADIATOR GAMES

For each fight, the gladiator types were usually mixed: hoplomachi fought Thraeces, and murmillos fought retiarii, and so on. This made the fights more interesting. People cheered for their favorite type of gladiator as well as for their favorite individual. Sometimes many pairs of gladiators, spaced out around the arena floor, fought at the same time. Other times a special pair of fighters would have the arena to themselves. Frequently, organ music filled the arena during the games, like the background soundtrack of a movie or the traditional organ music familiar to fans of American major league baseball.

The organ was invented in the third century B.C. In this Roman mosaic, an organist plays in the musical ensemble accompanying a raging gladiator fight.

Since each gladiator was fighting for his life, the fighting was desperate and savage. When one gladiator killed another, the fight was over. But when a gladiator was wounded, he could raise a finger as a plea for mercy. The highest ranking official in the arena, usually the emperor, could then spare the gladiator's life—or deny his request.

The emperor sometimes listened to the crowd when making his decision. If they did not like the defeated fighter, they told the emperor by pressing their thumbs against their own chests—the signal to put a sword through the fallen gladiator's heart. If the gladiator had fought well and the crowd liked him, they waved handkerchiefs and pointed their thumbs down—indicating the winner should drop his sword. The emperor used the same signals to tell the winning gladiator what to do.

A victorious gladiator looks to the audience for direction as to whether to kill or spare his opponent.

Representatives of the Roman god Mercury haul corpses from the arena.

Defeated gladiators whose lives were spared returned to the arena to fight on another day.

Sometimes a fallen gladiator pretended to be dead, but this rarely worked as a way to escape death. At the conclusion of every gladiator match, men dressed like Charon, the Etruscan demon of the underworld, entered the arena. Charon was the only remaining reference to the sport's Etruscan roots. The job of these men was to apply hot irons to the fallen bodies to make sure they were dead. Any fakers exposed in this fashion promptly had their throats cut.

Men dressed as the god Mercury (the transporter of the dead) then entered the arena and dragged the corpses away. Young boys cleaned up the bloodstains and raked fresh sand into place, and the next round of games began.

MORE ENTERTAINMENT

A day of gladiator games often included dramatic performances. Greek tragedies and myths were acted out with condemned criminals playing the parts. For instance, the myth of Orpheus, a young man who was able to charm wild animals by playing his flute, was acted out with a criminal playing the part of Orpheus. Instead of charming the wild beasts, however, he was devoured by them. Likewise, the myth of Icarus (a boy who made wings of wax and feathers that melted when he flew too close to the sun, causing him to plummet to earth) was enacted—with a real person falling to his death. Other spectacles included a bull that seemed to fly and an antelope that stopped and bowed before the emperor even as it was being chased by dogs.

The Romans also liked to see fantastic mechanical devices during a spectacle. One particular favorite was an enormous mechanical whale whose jaws opened to disgorge dozens of animals into the arena for a wild beast hunt. Dozens of people worked behind the scenes at any spectacle, working the mechanical devices and moving props into place.

Perhaps the most amazing production of all was the fantastic sea battle at the end of the first day of Titus's opening games. Millions of gallons of water were pumped into the arena. Specially trained horses and bulls swam into the arena, followed by small ships manned by crews of gladiators dressed as sailors. As the audience watched in amazement, the "sailor" gladiators fought to the death, reenacting a historic bloody naval battle. Accounts from that era indicate that the sea battle was the highlight of the opening day.

The first gladiator games held at the Flavian Amphitheater were the most extravagant, expensive games Romans had ever seen. On the opening day alone, Romans cheered on the deaths of more than five thousand animals. And the opening day was only the beginning. For one hundred days—more than three months—the festivities at the Colosseum continued all day, every day. During the course of these games, more than one thousand men and nine thousand animals were killed.

Mock sea battles were a popular form of entertainment in the Roman empire for centuries. Some arenas were built solely for this water sport.

Chapter Six
THE LAST OF THE FLAVIANS

(81–96)

When Mount Vesuvius erupted violently in A.D. 79, few of Pompeii's twenty thousand residents had time to escape. Burning hot ashes, cinders, and smoke filled the air.

BESIDES HOSTING GLADIATOR games and providing strong military leadership, Titus also displayed genuine concern for the Roman people. When Mount Vesuvius erupted, burying the city of Pompeii, Titus journeyed to the region, visited with the survivors, and established a fund to help them rebuild. After a fire swept through Rome, he ordered all the ornamentation stripped from his own palace and villas and redistributed to public buildings that had been damaged in the blaze. When a plague struck Rome, Titus donated his own money to fund medical aid

for the victims. The historian Suetonius wrote that Titus's concern for his people was "that of a parent for his injured children."

But Titus never got a chance to prove how great an emperor he might have become. In September A.D. 81, only twenty-six months into his reign, he died unexpectedly at the age of forty-one of a sudden and unexplained fever. A few writings from the time accuse his younger brother, Domitian, of killing him, but there is no real evidence that Titus was murdered. He most likely died of natural causes. The task of finishing the amphitheater fell to Domitian, who became the new emperor (reigning from A.D. 81 to 96).

Like his father, Vespasian, Domitian was nearly bald. But unlike his father, Domitian was vain. He apparently commanded official portrait painters and sculptors to portray him with flowing hair. Domitian was as hated by Romans as his father and brother were beloved. While Vespasian had been evenhanded and never held grudges, Domitian was tyrannical and vindictive. While Titus had been kind and generous,

Domitian was cruel and suspicious. Senators who disagreed with him were put to death. But regardless of his temperament, he knew the importance of the Flavian Amphitheater.

THE BASEMENT

Domitian is credited with adding an underground level beneath the arena, where gladiators and other participants, such as convicts and wild animals in cages, waited until it was time to fight. Like actors in a play, they needed a backstage area—a place where the audience wouldn't see them.

To create this space, workers dug out the ground beneath the arena floor. Then they built passages and rooms with walls of brick-faced concrete. To

Centuries ago the wooden arena floor was either recycled or rotted away, exposing features beneath it to the weather.

make these walls, bricklayers constructed two brick walls, then poured concrete between them. Eventually, this portion of the building was honeycombed with passages and rooms. Star gladiators may have had their own rooms. Criminals were usually lumped together in large cells.

When the walls were finished, the underground area was roofed with a wooden ceiling, then covered with a layer of sand to recreate the floor of the arena. Before this area was built, animals and gladiators and other players entered the arena through the west entrance. From the new underground space, participants emerged through trap doors in the floor. When it was time to go on, beasts were herded up ramps or hauled to the arena floor in mechanical elevators. Humans walked up ramps or stairs.

A CRUEL STREAK

Domitian was a great fan of the gladiator games, and with the magnificent Flavian Amphitheater at his disposal, he staged them often. By the end of his reign, he was spending most of his time and energy on the games.

The gladiator games brought out a cruel streak in Domitian. Because his brother Titus had favored the Thraeces, or light fighters, Domitian favored the "heavies," such as the hoplomachi or the murmillos. Domitian expected the crowd to support his favorites and used his power as emperor to

Of the character of Domitian (above), Suetonius wrote, "Reduced to financial straits by the cost of his buildings and shows. . . he had no hesitation in resorting to every sort of robbery. The property of the living and the dead was seized everywhere on any charge brought by any accuser. It was enough to allege any action or word derogatory to the majesty of the princeps [emperor]."

Domitian preferred the more heavily armored class of gladiators *(above).*

reinforce these preferences. Suetonius, a historian who was a teenager during Domitian's reign, recorded the fate of one hapless member of the Flavian Amphitheater's audience: "He had a head of a household dragged down at the games into the arena and thrown to the dogs because he had said that a 'Thracian' was the equal of a net-fighter but was not a match for the giver of the gladiatorial show. On him was a placard: 'A Thracian fan who spoke impiously.'"

As Domitian's obsession grew, he spent wildly. At his urging, the existing gladiator schools were taken over by the state. In addition, he founded four new gladiator schools in Rome.

GLADIATOR SCHOOLS

Gladiator schools were located throughout the empire. They were usually close to an arena and were run like military boarding schools. Each school had a series of barracks, a training square, a mess hall, work areas, a hospital, and a prison. The schools also kept busy staffs of tailors, armor makers, cobblers, metalworkers, masseurs, doctors, and others.

Newly arrived gladiators started with a general training course that lasted several months. Using wooden swords, they practiced standard thrusts.

WOMEN GLADIATORS

Gladiators were generally men, but women also fought as gladiators. The Romans were fond of unusual acts, such as a lion catching a rabbit in its mouth unharmed or an elephant walking a tightrope. Women gladiators were always a favorite.

Women gladiators first gained popularity during the reign of Nero. Domitian was the next emperor who really promoted them in the arena. He liked to pair them in fights against male dwarfs. Fights featuring women gladiators were sandwiched in between male gladiator fights, as were acrobats and clowns. Most women gladiators came from the lower classes, although a few were of noble birth.

Women gladiators appeared frequently in arenas throughout the empire until the reign of the emperor Septimius Severus. In A.D. 200 he banned women gladiator fights. For the next two hundred years, only men fought gladiator fights.

This Roman relief found in modern Turkey praises women gladiators Amazon and Achillea. The inscription also mentions "an honorable release from the arena"—probably for years of outstanding performances.

They also practiced parries against wooden figures. Retired gladiators trained and watched each recruit carefully to see what fighting style best suited him. Recruits were then broken into groups and given specialized trainers. Those who were going to be heavy fighters received different instruction than those who were going to be light fighters. During specialized training, the recruits fought each other instead of wooden figures.

After months of training and careful observation, the recruits were given real weapons. This precaution wasn't just for the safety of the recruits. Many of them were there against their will. Putting real weapons in their hands was risky because they might try to revolt or escape.

Only after years of rigorous training did recruits become gladiators and enter the arena. They might survive, even win freedom or fortune, or be able to train future gladiators back at their school. Gladiators who survived five years were set free. But the odds were against them. Few survived.

Rome's four gladiator schools were located directly east of the Flavian Amphitheater. The Ludus Dacicus and the Ludus Gallicus trained

HISTORIC GLADIATOR REVOLT: THE SPARTACUS REBELLION

In 73 B.C. Spartacus, a student in a gladiator school near Pompeii, organized a breakout. Spartacus had been sentenced to become a gladiator after deserting the Roman army. Armed with kitchen knives, he and seventy others battled their way out of the school, defeated the soldiers pursuing them, and escaped into the surrounding hills. They hid out in the inactive crater of Mount Vesuvius.

When Roman soldiers attacked them in the crater, Spartacus and his men fled by climbing down sheer rock cliffs on ladders made from vines. Spartacus's spirited fight for freedom won the respect of the people in the surrounding countryside. As Roman soldiers pursued his group across the countryside, many slaves, shepherds, and herdsmen joined them. Eventually their numbers reached more than six thousand. On nine different occasions, they defeated the Roman soldiers sent to capture them.

It took two years to put down the Spartacus rebellion, but in 71 B.C. Roman soldiers finally managed to trap the group in southern Italy. Spartacus was killed in the ensuing battle, and his army was destroyed.

gladiators that represented the Dacian and Gallic national fighting styles and armor types. The Ludus Matutinus trained fighters for the venationes. The Ludus Magnus trained all other types of gladiators. Of the four, the Ludus Magnus was the largest and most important.

The Ludus Magnus was run like a prestigious military camp. It was such an integral part of the Flavian Amphitheater that it was attached to the arena's underground chambers by an underground tunnel. Gladiators from the Ludus Magnus entered the arena directly from their barracks.

THE LAST FLAVIAN

Domitian ruled for fifteen years, nearly three years longer than the reigns of his father and brother combined. By the end of his reign in A.D. 96, he was so despised that his friends and servants—with the consent of his wife—assassinated him. Stephanus, a servant, said that he had news of a conspiracy and was admitted to Domitian's private rooms. While Domitian (fresh from his evening bath) scanned the list of supposed conspirators, Stephanus stabbed him. Several other assassins (all of them friends or servants) were also involved. Suetonius tells of his death:

> Domitian put up a good fight. The boy who was attending to the household gods in the bedroom witnessed the murder and later described it. . . . On receiving the first blow, Domitian grappled with Stephanus, and screamed at the boy to hand him the dagger which was kept under his pillow and then run for help; the dagger, however, proved to have no blade, and the doors to the servants' quarters were locked. Domitian fell on top of Stephanus and, after cutting his own fingers in an effort to disarm him, began clawing at his eye; but succumbed to seven further stabs, his assailants being a subaltern named Clodianus, Parthenius's freedman Maximus, Satur a head-chamberlain, and one of the Imperial gladiators. He died at the age of forty-four, on September 18th, A.D. 96.

Because of Domitian's extravagance, the empire was, once again, on the brink of bankruptcy. Domitian left no heir and with his death, the Flavian dynasty ended. The most lasting legacy of the Flavian dynasty would be the Flavian Amphitheater.

Chapter Seven

THE AMPHITHEATER THROUGH TIME

(96–modern times)

FROM THE DAY IT OPENED, the Flavian Amphitheater was a huge part of Roman life. Emperors for years to come—whether they approved of the games, as most of them did, or disapproved, as a few did—continued to sponsor gladiator games in the amphitheater, and Romans continued to flock to them. Hadrian, a well-educated and cultured emperor (who reigned from 117 to 138), organized games to mark many cele-

The Roman emperor Hadrian built a famous villa in Tivoli, Italy. In the tradition of other Roman building feats, the villa was massive. Its thirty buildings covered at least 250 acres (100 hectares).

brations, including his birthday. His successor, Antoninus Pius, also organized shows and is known as the first sponsor to introduce hyenas into the games. Marcus Aurelius (who reigned from A.D. 161 to 180) did not care for the games but staged them anyway. He did not want to upset the people.

The wanton bloodshed in the arena brought out the worst in a few emperors. Commodus (who reigned from A.D. 177 to 192) was so fascinated with the arena that he had his own private quarters at Ludus Magnus, the gladiator school next door. He fought as a gladiator more than one thousand times. He was known to slice off the noses or ears of his opponents, and even to kill them. Because he was the emperor, opponents didn't dare harm him. On one occasion he cut off the head of an ostrich with one clean swipe of his sword and then approached some senators who were sitting in the podium. Historians say

Lightning struck the Flavian Amphitheater in A.D. 217, causing a tremendously destructive fire.

he smiled in a threatening way and lifted the bird's head in one hand and his sword in the other and waved them at the senators. This apparently was a hint to the senators that the same thing could happen to them if Commodus did not like them.

LIGHTNING AND FIRE
IN THE FLAVIAN AMPHITHEATER

By A.D. 200, the Flavian Amphitheater had been housing games for well over one hundred years. It was an important landmark in Rome. With so much stone and concrete in the structure, it appeared indestructible. But it was not. During a storm in 217, the building was struck repeatedly by lightning. The upper tier of the building, which was made of wood, blazed. Even though the rain came down heavily and firefighters doused the blaze with additional water from the town's water systems, they could not put out the fire. The flames heated the stone portions to such a degree that they cracked when water hit them. The metal clamps that held the blocks together exploded. The enormous columns from the top of the building tumbled down the cavea, crushing the marble, concrete, and stone in their path. When these flaming pieces of the top level reached the arena, the fire was further fed by the wooden structures of the underground chambers.

After this fire the Flavian Amphitheater was unusable. Little more than the most basic framework was left. Most of the huge task of rebuilding Rome's most beloved monument fell to the emperors Elagabalus (who reigned from 218 to 222) and Alexander Severus (who reigned from 222 to 235). The amphitheater reopened in 222 after five years of reconstruction, but it was not completely restored for another fifteen years. In all, reconstruction took about twenty years. Elagabalus, who was a great fan of the gladiator games, staged lavish celebrations that included lotteries. Lottery winners received such prizes as live bears and pounds of gold. Coins featuring the Flavian Amphitheater's image were minted in 238, probably to mark the completed restoration of the building.

Repairs to the Flavian Amphitheater were already under way when Alexander Severus (above) became the emperor of Rome. The restoration continued several years after his thirteen-year reign ended.

THE CHRISTIANS AND THE END OF THE GAMES

In A.D. 249 a man named Decius became emperor (reigning until 251). One of the first things Decius did was to order all Roman citizens to make a sacrifice to one of the many Roman gods. Those who did not risked torture and execution. In spite of the risk, a number of people refused to make the sacrifice. To them the Roman religion was wrong.

Their religion, Christianity, had begun to take hold around A.D. 50. Christians were often persecuted because they worshiped a single god, refusing to acknowledge the many Roman gods. Nero had distrusted Christians so much that he accused them of starting the great fire that devastated Rome. He had ordered many burned alive.

When Christians would not make sacrifices to the Roman gods, Decius ordered them punished harshly. Fabianus (Saint Fabian), a Christian bishop (high-ranking church official), was killed. Many others were too. Anti-Christian feelings led to riots in some parts of the empire. At least two Christian men are known to have been executed in the arena of the Flavian Amphitheater. Probably many others were also killed there. Later emperors also persecuted Christians. But Decius, who ruled for only about a year and a half, is the emperor remembered for killing them in the Flavian Amphitheater, permanently staining the building's legacy.

> Later emperors also persecuted Christians. But Decius, who ruled for only about a year and a half, is the emperor remembered for killing them in the Flavian Amphitheater, permanently staining the building's legacy.

It is impossible to know how many Christians were killed by the Romans. But despite the persecution, Christianity continued to catch hold and grow. In 313 the emperor Constantine (who reigned from 306 to 337) issued an edict granting Christians religious freedom. In 326 he banned gladiator matches. Finally, in 327 he himself converted to Christianity.

In spite of Constantine's ban, gladiator games continued illegally in many parts of the empire. But the games were expensive to put on, and the empire was not as prosperous as it once had been. The games were less frequent and less grand than they had been. After 330 Constantine moved the capital of the empire to Constantinople (Istanbul, Turkey, in modern times), and by the end of the century, the empire was split into the West Roman Empire and the East Roman Empire. The people of Rome were besieged by hunger and disease. All these things probably made the Flavian Amphitheater seem less important to the Romans. In the second half of the fourth century, parts of the building (such as some of the marble fountains) were stripped away to be used elsewhere. Maintenance was neglected until much of the water system and some of the bathrooms no longer worked.

DAMAGE AND RECONSTRUCTION

The building and Rome itself suffered more damage in the following decades. From A.D. 408 to 410, a group of invaders called the Visigoths ravaged and looted the city, then took control of it. The Flavian Amphitheater was badly damaged, but Rome's Visigoth conquerors staged venationes and wrestling matches there anyway. In 416 the Romans drove the Visigoths away, and by 423 they had restored the amphitheater once again. Games were probably held there once again, too.

Visigoth soldiers from southwestern France further damaged the Colosseum when they conquered Rome.

Neptune, shown in this third-century Roman mosaic, was known to the Romans as the god of earthquakes. In modern times, earthquakes remain frequent in Italy, posing an ongoing threat to the Flavian Amphitheater.

However, in 429 and 443 earthquakes shook the city and seriously damaged the Flavian Amphitheater. The sewers were probably blocked, causing flooding of the arena. Much of the highest level of seating fell down, and chunks of the building tumbled down the cavea and into the arena. The Romans decided to repair the building yet again, indicating that games were still important. When the building was restored this time, the underground chambers were partly filled in.

A second group of invaders called the Vandals sacked the city in 455 and again in 472. Each of these attacks forced thousands of Romans to flee the city. While Rome may have been home to as many as one million people in the middle 300s, it held only about one hundred thousand in the late 400s. The West Roman Empire—where Rome was—was conquered by a German general named Odoacer in 476. The popularity of gladiator games was at an all-time low. By the end of the century, it is possible that the Flavian Amphitheater's arena and the lowest rows of seats were the only parts of the building still being maintained and used.

In either 484 or 508 a massive earthquake—so destructive it was nicknamed the *abominandus* ("dreadful")—struck the city. This quake left much of the Flavian Amphitheater in complete collapse and the rest dangerously unstable. City officials had unstable parts knocked down and removed along with the rest of the debris. Any columns that remained along the top were slid down the cavea, into the arena, and buried in the underground chambers.

These repairs made the amphitheater safe enough to hold venationes once again. Gladiator games had become unacceptable and were no longer held. The last venationes (and last of any games) known to be held in the Flavian Amphitheater were in 523. By this time the Flavian Amphitheater was already being used more as a quarry than an amphitheater.

Spanish artist Hubert Robert painted later quarrying activities at the Flavian Amphitheater. He made sketches for this painting while in Italy in 1754.

> "While stands the Colosseum, Rome shall stand. When falls the Colosseum, Rome shall fall. When Rome falls, the world shall fall."
>
> **—Bede's recording of a Latin saying**

Valuable building materials in the structure were abundant, including tons of travertine and tufa, marble, iron clamps, lead pipes, and bricks. Builders freely removed these materials from the building and used them to build other structures.

During the first half of the sixth century, the population of Rome was down to the tens of thousands. Famine and disease wiped out most of these remaining people, and by 545 no more than five hundred people still lived in the city. The Flavian Amphitheater was barred and closed to the public. Still, thieves broke in and stole metals and building supplies. Many people found ways to get inside and lived there illegally, building shelters and keeping animals. The magnificent barrel-vaulted walkways of the Flavian Amphitheater were used as stables for sheep and pigs and other animals. By 700 grass grew on the cavea and shrubbery sprouted from Level 4.

Many European Christians made their way to Rome on pilgrimages in the 700s. Pilgrims returning to Britain from Rome brought a popular Latin saying with them. Bede, a British historian at that time, recorded it:

Quandiu stabit coliseus, stabit et Roma;
Quando cadet coliseus, cadet et Roma;
Quando cadet Roma, cadet et mundus.

In modern times the most common English translation is:

While stands the Colosseum, Rome shall stand.
When falls the Colosseum, Rome shall fall.
When Rome falls, the world shall fall.

This may be one of the earliest examples of the name of the Colossus, the statue which long stood next to the Flavian Amphitheater, being transferred to the amphitheater. *Coliseus* in Latin is masculine, implying Bede meant the statue, while *colosseum* is neuter.

Around the end of the ninth and the beginning of the tenth century, the land around the Flavian Amphitheater filled with settlers again. The church of Santa Maria Nova, a Catholic church, owned the land. Deeds to the land refer to the Flavian Amphitheater as the "Amphitheatrum Colosseum." Over time, the building came to be known simply as the Colosseum, although the statue no longer exists.

The Colossus *(pictured at the left in this sketch)* first gave its name to the Flavian Amphitheater about one thousand years after it was built.

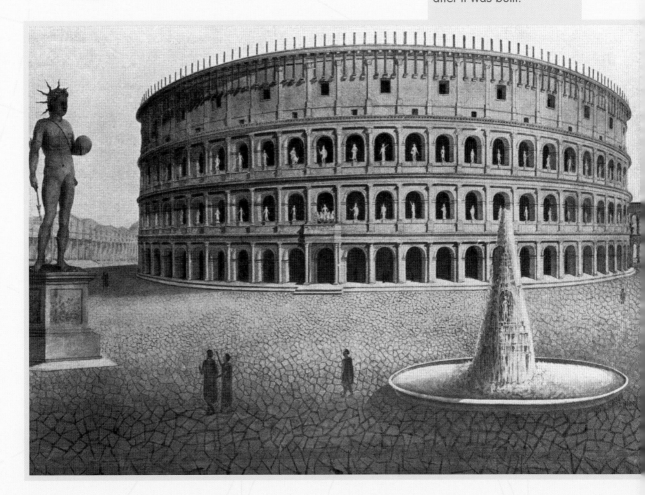

DEMOLISHING AND SAVING THE PAST

By the fourteenth century, the Roman Catholic Church had become very powerful. And the city of Rome had experienced a renewal.

It had been about eight hundred years since any games had been held in the Colosseum. What the Colosseum had been used for in ancient times was no longer common knowledge. Even so, the Church saw the amphitheater as a symbol of the ancient Roman Empire, a civilization that had worshiped many gods and persecuted Christians.

No wonder that the Church itself quarried all but the north face of the facade for building materials. Pope Nicholas V (pope from 1447 to 1455) pillaged the Colosseum's stone for use in buildings such as Saint Peter's Basilica in Rome. Pope Nicholas had more than two thousand cartloads of stone hauled away from the Colosseum in a single year.

Saint Peter's Basilica *(below)*. is the pope's cathedral in Vatican City near Rome. It has undergone many renovations. Records from 1460 to 1462 show workers used travertine from the Colosseum to construct a new piazza and stairs for the basilica.

IN·HONOREM·PRINCIPIS·APOST·PAVLVS·V·BVRGHESIVS·ROMAN   ·IT·MAX·AN·MDCXII·PONT·V

A successor, Pope Alexander VI (pope from 1492 to 1503), leased the building to others who quarried stone for a church, two palaces, and several bridges in Rome.

At the same time a group of intellectuals called humanists—who were interested in studying ancient history and art, including architecture—were studying the building (and other ancient monuments in Rome). They used what they learned as a basis for their own architecture. One of them, a man named Flavio Biondo, was the first person to understand that the amphitheater had been used for gladiator games. The humanists were saddened by the condition of the Colosseum, and they argued with Church leaders over their decision to take apart the building, piece by piece.

Later popes wanted to preserve the Colosseum but found it too costly. Pope Sixtus V (1585 to 1590) tried to turn the building into a cloth factory, and Pope Clement IX (1667 to 1669) used the Colosseum as a warehouse for a nearby gunpowder factory.

Yet in 1743 a partial remodeling of the Colosseum was begun. The following year Pope Benedict XIV (pope from 1740 to 1758) forbade the removal of any more stones from the building. By then the building was regarded as an important monument, and no more looting or living there was allowed. Pope Benedict erected an enormous cross on the arena floor in memory of the Christians he believed had died there, and he declared the building a public church.

Pope Benedict XIV called a stop to quarrying the Colosseum for building materials.

> "I was amazed that the Romans, who have such a taste in all things, could have allowed such a slaughter. Modern intervention has ruined those wonderful monuments."
> —François-Marius Granet

A TOURIST ATTRACTION

By the mid-1700s, Rome was one of the greatest tourist attractions in Europe. People were fascinated by the ruins of the Roman Empire. The city became a magnet for writers and artists.

The Colosseum and its surroundings were excavated in 1805 and again in 1828. The second excavation led to the discoveries of the base of the Colossus, the pavement of an ancient street, and a cemetery. In 1806 after an earthquake damaged the building, construction was begun on large buttresses (support structures) of brick and travertine to help hold up the east side. In 1826 buttresses on the west side were completed.

Throughout the middle of the century, different parts of the Colosseum were rebuilt, including some underground passages and several arches and floors. But not everyone approved of the methods employed. After observing engineers at work on the Colosseum in 1829, artist François-Marius Granet wrote, "I was amazed that the Romans, who have such a taste in all things, could have allowed such a slaughter. Modern intervention has ruined those wonderful monuments."

In 1861 the nation of Italy was created, and in 1870 it instituted the Office of the Superintendent of the Excavation and Preservation of Monuments for the purpose of actively excavating and studying ancient monuments—especially the Colosseum. The following year the vegetation was cleared away from the building, and people could finally see the structure for the first time in more than one thousand years. In 1874 and 1875 a team of archaeologists excavated the center of the Colosseum, revealing the rooms, passages, and cages beneath the arena floor. They also found nearby pits containing the stinking remains of thousands of animals and gladiators. The stench of death still lingered in these mass graves.

FLOWERS AND TREES IN THE COLOSSEUM

In the 1800s, botanists became interested in the Colosseum. Centuries of neglect had left the building looking more like a work of nature than a work of humans. Cherry, elm, pear, and fig trees had sprouted on its highest ledges. Wild roses, clematis, and ivy climbed over the walls. And the stonework in the building was covered with daisies, marigolds, strawberries, violets, sage, and hundreds of other plants.

Rome was full of ruins, most of them covered with some vegetation. What made the Colosseum unique was that many of its plants were found nowhere else in Rome or even in Europe. It was a storehouse of exotic plants.

The first comprehensive study of the Colosseum's flora was done in 1831 by Antonio Sebastiani. He identified 261 different species of plants growing in the Colosseum. In 1855 an Englishman named Richard Deakin identified 420 different species of plants in the building. Deakin published the results of his study in a beautifully illustrated book titled *Flora of the Colosseum.*

Many botanists speculated that the seeds of these exotic plants had come into the Colosseum among the foodstuffs shipped in to feed the animals for the venationes. In 1871 Pietro Rosa, an archaeologist, was given permission to clear out all the vegetation and study the structure of the ruin.

Weeding the Colosseum remains an ongoing struggle in modern times.

The research of 1874 and 1875 had to be cut short due to flooding in the underground chambers. An ancient sewer was discovered in 1879. It was then connected to the sewers of the Colosseum, which kept the area dry. In 1892 several radial walls and piers were reconstructed.

In the early 1900s, the monument was not treated as well. Sloppy excavations and reconstructions (made of asphalt) distorted the original shape of the structure. Political groups rallied and sometimes rioted there, destroying some columns and capitals. Streets were built very close to the Colosseum, subjecting it to traffic pollution, and parking was even permitted inside the building. Later, a subway tunnel was cut into the foundation on the west side, damaging the drainage system and leading to serious flooding. During World War II (1939 to 1945), the Colosseum was used for shelter and the storage of weapons by German paratroopers.

In 1930, Italian dictator Benito Mussolini *(far left, on horseback)* addresses a crowd in the Colosseum celebrating the eighth anniversary of his Fascist government. Leaders of both Italy and Germany, allies in World War II, promoted themselves as modern heirs of the Roman Empire.

In the following years the building received enough maintenance to keep it open to visitors but just barely. In the 1970s the first scientifically conducted archaeological studies were undertaken. More restoration work was done, and this time the work sought to preserve the ancient structure's original design. Excavations in the sewers turned up a great deal of information about the building's history. Also in the 1970s, city officials restricted traffic around the Colosseum.

In the 1970s, the first scientifically conducted archaeological studies were undertaken. More restoration work was done, and this time the work sought to preserve the ancient structure's original design.

THE COLOSSEUM IN MODERN TIMES

Only about 15 percent of the Colosseum was open to the public in 1992. The rest of the building was too dangerous. Sections of floor were missing, bricks were loose, and no one knew if the stones were stable. That year the Italian government allocated $19.3 million toward a restoration of the building. In 2002 the Colosseum neared the end of that project, its greatest restoration project ever. The underground chambers were excavated more fully and have been opened to tourists. People may walk through this portion of the Colosseum and see where prisoners, gladiators, and animals waited before they were sent above to fight for their lives. At one end of the arena, a narrow walkway has been constructed across the top of the underground chambers, allowing people to view them from directly above.

The most visible part of the restoration project was the rebuilding of a portion of the arena floor. The restoration of the arena floor protects some of the underground area from further damage. But less than one-half of the arena floor has been restored. The rest of the floor (aside from the small viewing walkway) is still missing, leaving the underground area visible from above.

Tourists enjoy the rebuilt arena floor and central walkway crossing the long axis of the Colosseum.

A less visible but much more difficult job was stabilizing the Colosseum's foundation by realigning its supporting stones and shoring up of its exterior arches. Centuries of wars, earthquakes, and fires had left the Colosseum skewed and crumbling. A widening crack in the north face of the building threatened to split open the exterior wall. Construction workers coaxed gigantic blocks of ancient travertine and tufa back into their original positions, millimeter by millimeter.

An indoor museum has been opened on Level 2, and roughly 35 percent of the building is open to the public. Restorers hope to open all of the Colosseum eventually.

The Colosseum was built as a place to hold gladiator games, games that brought out the worst in the Roman people. But the games stopped more than sixteen hundred years ago. And the Colosseum still stands. Throughout most of its existence, the Colosseum has been put to many other uses besides gladiator games.

Vespasian and his son Titus would probably be pleased. They built the amphitheater to establish themselves as powerful emperors and to win the support of the Roman people. They wanted to demonstrate the grandeur and power of the Roman Empire. And they wanted to make sure that people remembered the Flavian family. A verse that poet Marcus Valerius Martialis, or Martial, wrote for the opening of the Flavian Amphitheater still rings true:

> "Every work yields to the Imperial Amphitheatre. Posterity will speak of this one work instead of all others."
> —**Martial**

Let the barbarian wonders of the Pyramids of Memphis [Egypt] be silent, and don't let the Assyrians boast of the labour of building Babylon. Don't praise the soft Ionians for the temple of Diana. . . . Every work yields to the Imperial Amphitheatre. Posterity will speak of this one work instead of all others.

Titus had a coin featuring the Colosseum minted in A.D. 80 to celebrate completion of the grand building. It has been featured on many coins since then. *Left,* in 2002 Italy selected the Colosseum to represent Italian culture on one of the first euro coins minted.

A Timeline of the Colosseum

264 B.C. Gladiators fight at the funeral of Decimus Brutus Pera, marking the first known Roman gladiator games.

90 B.C. Gladiator games are being staged in Rome in circuses and forums.

80 B.C. The earliest permanent amphitheater known to historians is constructed in Pompeii.

73 B.C. Spartacus and his followers escape from a gladiator school. They survive numerous attacks from soldiers sent to capture them before Spartacus is killed in 71 B.C.

29 B.C. Titus Statilius Taurus builds Rome's first amphitheater.

A.D. 50 Christianity begins to take hold in the Roman Empire.

54 Nero comes to power.

64 A great fire starts in the Circus Maximus and ravages Rome for six days.

67 Nero's Golden House is completed.

68 The Year of the Four Emperors. Nero commits suicide and Galba takes power. Galba is overthrown by Otho, who, in turn, is overthrown by Vitellius.

69 Vespasian is proclaimed emperor on December 20.

ca. 75 Construction on the Flavian Amphitheater begins.

79 Though construction on the amphitheater is not quite finished, Vespasian dedicates it. He dies on June 23, and Titus becomes emperor. Near Pompeii, Mout Vesuvius erupts.

80 Titus opens the Flavian Amphitheater with a gala one-hundred-day celebration, including venationes, gladiator games, and a naval battle.

81 Titus dies of a fever in September. Domitian becomes emperor.

96 Domitian is murdered, and the Flavian dynasty (ruling family) ends.

177–192 The reign of Commodus, who fought in the Flavian Amphitheater as a gladiator

217 Much of the Flavian Amphitheater is destroyed after it is struck by lightning and burns.

222 The amphitheater is reopened after some restoration.

249 Decius becomes emperor and kills Christians in the amphitheater.

326 Constantine bans gladiator games, but because of their popularity they continue to be held illegally in some parts of the empire.

Construction of Level 2

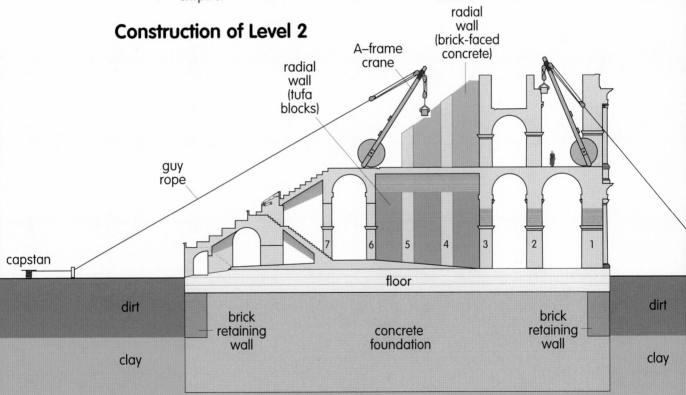

330 The capital of the Roman Empire is moved to Constantinople (Istanbul in modern-day Turkey). By the end of the century, the empire has been divided into the West Roman Empire and the East Roman Empire.

408–410 The Visigoths take control of Rome, badly damaging the Flavian Amphitheater during their conquest and occupation of the city.

416 The Romans drive out the Visigoths.

455 Invaders called the Vandals sack Rome.

472 The Vandals sack Rome a second time.

476 The West Roman Empire is conquered by Odoacer.

484 or 508 A massive earthquake, known as abominandus, hits Rome and devastates the Flavian Amphitheater. Officials rebuild it enough to hold small crowds for venationes.

523 The last known venationes (and last of any games) are held in the amphitheater.

ca. 900 People again begin to settle the area around the Flavian Amphitheater, which is known by this time as the Amphitheatrum Colosseum.

1400s The Colosseum is quarried for building materials.

1744 Pope Benedict XIV forbids removal of any more stones from the Colosseum.

1805 & 1828 The Colosseum and its surroundings are excavated.

1861 The nation of Italy is created.

1874–1875 The arena is excavated, revealing the underground rooms and passages. A mass grave for animals and gladiators is also discovered.

1892 Several radial walls are reconstructed.

1930s   Reconstruction of a Colosseum seating section takes place. A subway tunnel is cut into the foundation of the Colosseum, damaging the drainage system. The remains of the Meta Sudans fountain at the Colosseum are removed for road construction.

1939–1945   German paratroopers use the Colosseum during World War II.

1970s   The first scientifically conducted archaeological studies are done on the Colosseum, and traffic is restricted from the area.

1992   The Italian government allocates $19.3 million toward a restoration of the Colosseum.

2002   The restoration project, the greatest the Colosseum has ever had, is nearly finished. A museum opens on the second floor, and more than 35 percent of the Colosseum is open to the public.

Sources Notes

Acknowledgments for quoted material: p. 16, as quoted in Cornelius Tacitus, *The Annals,* Book IV, trans. Alfred John Church and William Jackson Brodribb (New York: The Modern Library, 1942) and reprinted on the web at Joakim Hansson, Luleå Tekniska Universitet, Sweden, "A bit of Swedish (and scandinavic) history," May 30, 1999, <http://www.luth.se/luth/present/sweden/history/lit/tacitus/annals.iv.html>; pp. 18, 19 (top), as quoted in D. L. Bomgardner, *The Story of the Roman Amphitheater* (London: Routledge, 2000; pp. 19 (bottom), 47, 63, 69, as quoted in Peter Quennell and the Editors of Newsweek Book Division, *The Colosseum* (New York: Newsweek, 1971); p. 22, as quoted in Christopher Scarre, *Chronicle of the Roman Emperors: the Reign-by-Reign Record of the Rulers of Imperial Rome* (London: Thames and Hudson, 1995); p. 56, as quoted in Petronius, *The Satyricon,* 117.5, in Barbara McManus, "Arena: Gladiatorial Games," June 1999, <http://www.vroma.org/~bmcmanus/arena.html>; p. 56, as quoted in Ada Gabucci, ed., *The Colosseum,* trans. Mary Becker (Los Angeles: The J. Paul Getty Museum, 2001); p. 65, 66, Brian Jones and Robert Milnes, ed., *Suetonius: The Flavian Emporers—a Historical Commentary* (London: The Bristol Classical Press, 2002); p. 78, as attributed to Bede in *The Catholic Encyclopedia,* Volume IV (New York: Robert Appleton Company, 1908) and reprinted on line in "The Colosseum," *The Catholic Encyclopedia,* (Kevin Knight: 2002) <http://www.newadvent.org/cathen/04101b.htm>; p. 82, François-Marius Granet, 1829, as quoted by Andrea Pepe, Daniele Pepe, Catherine McElwee, "Romantic," *The Colosseum: a Site on the Roman Amphitheatre,* December, 2002 <http://www.the-colosseum.net/history/romantic.htm>; p. 87, Martial, *On the Spectacles,* 1, as translated by David Noy, "Living in the City of Rome 7: the Amphitheater," Department of Classics, University of Wales, Lampeter, December 21, 2001, <http://www.lamp.ac.uk/~noy/rome7.htm>.

Selected Bibliography

Beste, H. J. "Construction and Development Stages of the Wooden Arena Flooring of the Colosseum in Rome." United Nations Educational, Scientific and Cultural Organization, n.d. <http://www.unesco.org/archi2000/pdf/beste.pdf> (February 6, 2003).

Bomgardner, D. L. *The Story of the Roman Amphitheater.* London: Routledge, 2000.

Cerone, M., A. Viskovic, F. Fumagalli, and R. Rea. "The Re-Formation of Arena Floor Deck in the Colosseum in Roma." United Nations Educational, Scientific and Cultural Organization, n.d. <http://www.unesco.org/archi2000/pdf/cerone.pdf> (February 6, 2003).

Cerone, M., G. Groci, and A. Viskovic. "The Structural Behaviour of Colosseum over the Centuries." United Nations Educational, Scientific and Cultural Organization, n.d. <http://www.unesco.org/archi2000/pdf/crocicoloss.pdf> (February 6, 2003).

Como, M., U. Ianniruberto, M. Imbimbo, and F. Lauri. "Limit Analysis of the External Wall of Colosseum." United Nations Educational, Scientific and Cultural Organization, n.d. <http://www.unesco.org/archi2000/pdf/como.pdf> (February 6, 2003).

Connolly, Peter, and Hazel Dodge. *The Ancient City: Life in Classical Athens and Rome.* Oxford, England: Oxford University Press, 1998.

Deutsche Presse-Agentur. "Rome Colosseum Being Restored for Wider Public Viewing." *National Geographic.com,* June 29, 2001. <http://news.nationalgeographic.com/news/2001/06/0625_wirecoliseum.html> (February 6, 2003).

Gabucci, Ada, ed. *The Colosseum.* Translated by Mary Becker. Los Angeles: The J. Paul Getty Museum, 2001.

Jones, Brian, and Robert Milnes, eds. *Suetonius: The Flavian Emperors—A Historical Commentary.* London: The Bristol Classical Press, 2002.

Nadeau, Barbie. "Rebuilding the Colosseum," *Newsweek International,* September 10, 2001. <http://web.tiscali.it/no-redirect-tiscali/Colosseum/around/newsweek.htm> (February 6, 2003).

Pearson, John. *Arena: The Story of the Colosseum.* New York: McGraw-Hill Book Company, 1973.

Quennell, Peter, and the Editors of Newsweek Book Division. *The Colosseum.* New York: Newsweek, 1971.

"Spectacle Returns to the Colosseum," *BBC News,* July 20, 2000. <http://news.bbc.co.uk/2/hi/world/europe/842281.stm> (February 6, 2003).

Taylor, Rabun. *Roman Builders: A Study in Architectural Process.* Cambridge, MA: Cambridge University Press, 2003.

Wilson Jones, Mark. *Principles of Roman Architecture.* New Haven, CT: Yale University Press, 2000.

Further Reading and Websites

Barghusen, Joan. *Daily Life in Ancient and Modern Rome.* Minneapolis: Lerner Publications Company, 1999.
This colorful and fact-filled book combines descriptions of daily life and important historical events. Readers will learn about Roman religious life, entertainment, class divisions, and the military through the ages.

Burrell, Roy, and Peter Connolly. *The Romans.* Oxford, England: Oxford University Press, 1991.
Readers will find a wealth of information about Roman history and ancient Romans in this illustrated book.

Nardo, Don. *The Ancient Romans.* San Diego: Lucent Books, 2001.
This book describes the history of ancient Rome, from its founding to its decline and fall. It includes discussions of the ancient Romans' social classes and way of life.

Pepe, Andrea, Daniele Pepe, and Catherine McElwee. *The Colosseum,* n.d.
<http://www.the-colosseum.net/>
A wealth of information in both English and Italian on the history and use of the Colosseum from its construction through modern times may be found in this website, as well as helpful tips for tourists.

Ryan, T. M. M. *Dead Romans.* 1996–2001.
<http://www.deadromans.com>
This website offers information on the history, coins, art, and architecture of ancient Rome. Click on the building and take a virtual walkthrough of the Colosseum.

Woods, Michael, and Mary B. Woods. *Ancient Construction.* Minneapolis: Lerner Publications Company, 2000.
In this book, readers will learn how Romans built their roads, windows, and bathrooms, and they will discover how Romans invented concrete to aid in their construction of huge structures such as the Colosseum.

Index

Lesley A. DuTemple has written more than a dozen books for young readers, including many award-winning titles such as her biography *Jacques Cousteau,* winner of the National Science Teachers Association/Children's Book Council Outstanding Science Trade Books for Children. After graduating from the University of California, San Diego, she attended the University of Utah's Graduate School of Architecture, where she concentrated in design and architectural history. The creator of the **Great Building Feats** series, she believes, "There's a human story behind every one of these building feats, and those stories are just as amazing as the projects themselves."

Photo Acknowledgments

The images in this book are used with the permission of: © Michael Maslan Historic Photographs/CORBIS, p. 1; © Van der Heyden Collection/Independent Picture Service, pp. 2–3, 30–31, 37, 40-41, 45, 53, 64, 83, 87; © Alinari/Art Resource, NY, p. 4–5; © North Wind Picture Archives, pp., 8–9, 10, 19, 24; © Stock Montage, pp. 11, 60; © Bettmann/CORBIS, pp. 13, 57 (top), 65, 75, 79; © Gian Berto Vanni/CORBIS, pp. 15; © The Art Archive/Museo Capitolino Rome/Dagli Orti (A), p. 17; © Stapleton Collection/CORBIS, p. 20; © The Art Archive/Dagli Orti (A), p. 21; © The Art Archive/Museo della Civilta Romana Rome/Dagli Orti, pp. 23, 29, 36; © David Zimmerman/CORBIS, p. 26; © The Art Archive/Archaeological Museum Aquileia/Dagli Orti, p. 34; © Werner Foreman/Art Resource, NY, p. 35; © Scott Gilchrist/Archivision Inc., pp. 39, 48-49, 70-71, 80; © Tina M. Trumbower, p. 46; © Fototeca Unione, American Academy in Rome, p. 51; © Archivo Iconografico, S.A./CORBIS, pp. 54, 73; © Roger Wood/CORBIS, pp. 55, 58, 66, 76; © Pizzoli Alberto/CORBIS SYGMA, p. 57 (bottom); © Library of Congress (LC-USZ62-120862), p. 59; © Mary Evans Picture Library, p. 61; © The Art Archive/Museo di Capodimonte, Naples/Dagli Orti (A), p. 62–63; © The British Museum, p. 67; Corbis Royalty free, p. 72; © The Bridgeman Art Library, p. 77; © Christie's Images/CORBIS, p. 81; © Hulton-Deutsch Collection/CORBIS, p. 84; © Joan K. Mayer, p. 86. Maps and Diagrams on pp. 6, 27, 28, 32, 33, 38, 42, 44, 47, 50, 89 by Laura Westlund.

Cover photos are by Minneapolis Public Library (front) and The Art Archive/Archaeological Museum Naples/Dagli Orti (back).